THE NEW RELATIONSHIP

THE NEW RELATIONSHIP

Reclaiming the Freedom to Love without Fear

Allan Hardman

with
Jessica Varga McKay

Cover design by Suzanne Bastear.

ISBN 979-8-9937111-0-2

For Allan—

and all who loved him

Contents

Dream with Me

Dream with me.
Dream with me now.
Dream that you know the truth of who you are
    in this moment—right here, right now.
Open yourself to the truth that you are a
    divine expression in physical form, an
    expression of one amazing life-spirit pres-
    ence, alive as you.
Dream with me that in this divinity—this
    perfect part of a perfect whole—there is no
    expectation for you to be any different than
    you are.
There is no reason to judge yourself...
Knowing that in the perfection of this universe,
    every part is perfect.
And knowing that you *are part of this*
    universe, there is no place where perfection
    stops and you begin.

You are a perfect part of a perfect universe.
Dream with me right now as we call that
perfection, that awareness, that acceptance,
Love.
Dream Love for yourself.
Dream Love for this moment.
Dream Love for all of creation.
Dream with me that from this perfection, you
have no need or reason to justify anything
you are—anything you think, anything
you feel, anything you do.
Dream with me that knowing yourself as Love,
as that divine perfection, you have no need
to take care of anyone in order to be okay,
or to prove anything.
Dream with me that when you help, when you
reach out, when you touch others, you do
so not from obligation or fear...
But as a soul expression of your love and your
acceptance, as a human and as a divine,
perfect expression of life.
Dream with me that you understand and feel
the wholeness of yourself in relationships of
all kinds.
You carry that wholeness to others—not asking
them to complete you, not offering to
complete them—but recognizing the perfec-
tion and completeness of each individual.
You simply offer your presence as Love.
And dream with me that your love for yourself
—and for the divinity and perfection that

*you are—is so strong that you are willing
and able to express the truth of the unique
being that you are.*

*You express that truth—the truth of your feel-
ings, the truth that arises in you in each
moment—and you use it to guide your life.*

Dream this dream with me now.

Feel it in your body.

Feel it in your mind.

Feel it in your heart.

And dream with me the ultimate happiness.

*See, feel, and know yourself happy—not
because life never brings pain, but because
your nature as love pours out of you as
acceptance for all of creation.*

*Imagine yourself in the world with your heart
wide open, a beam of love and acceptance
pouring out of you.*

Feel the lightness in your step.

The ease in your body.

*The freedom to be you exactly as you came here
to be—exactly as you are in each moment.*

Dream this dream with me.

This is all there is.

This moment.

This love.

This truth.

— Allan Hardman, 2005

What If Your Life Is a Dream?

IN YOUR NIGHTMARE, YOU ARE RUNNING AND RUNNING... There is no way to escape. You feel fear pounding through your body. Suddenly you awaken, maybe drenched in sweat, and realize that it was only a dream.

You were dreaming it, it wasn't real, and you are safe.

Imagine with me now that your life is only a dream. Imagine that you are asleep in a different way, dreaming your life and projecting it out through your belief systems and agreements into a world that simply dreams it with you.

Perhaps your dream scares you. Or perhaps it seems out of your control—you are running and running, and there is nowhere to feel safe.

Now imagine what it would feel like to awaken and realize that it is not real... no more real than your night-mare. Imagine that you could awaken and discover that everything you believe and know to be true about life and the world is only a dream.

A long time ago, you were taught the dream of your life by the people who were here ahead of you, dreaming their dream of life together.

Imagine that you awaken and decide to become a master of your awareness, to discover what you believe to be true. You awaken from *their* dream, and begin to dream your *own* dream.

And you feel safe, maybe for the first time.

Awakening from the Nightmare

When I was 20 years old, I became engaged to the girl I'd been dating for over a year. I did not want to lose her love, and when she gave me an ultimatum, I asked her to marry me.

Our engagement was celebrated by our families and announced in the local newspaper. But as the following weeks and months passed, it became very clear to me that I did not want to marry her. I also did not want to be responsible for hurting her.

Yet even deeper than that was my own fear of rejection. I was afraid to tell her the truth, because the truth I would have to tell was the truth of who I really was and *what I felt*, and I believed that version of me was unlovable. It felt safer to be rejected for someone I *wasn't* than to risk being rejected for who I really was.

I postponed the wedding, hoping she would make the decision to break up with me. When that didn't work, I behaved badly, telling myself that if she rejected the "bad" version of me, I wouldn't have to face the guilt and fear I felt about hurting her by telling the truth.

But she didn't reject me. She kept forgiving me. And finally, with the wedding just weeks away, the truth of my feelings erupted.

She left the next day, and I never saw her again.

My fear of rejection and pattern of manipulating outcomes continued into my 30s and early 40s. I realized that my relationships weren't working, so I decided to find out why. I went to therapy and spent weeks and weeks pouring out my story. One day, my therapist asked, "How is therapy working for you?"

"I don't know," I said. "I thought you were supposed to tell *me* what's going on here. I'm just telling you my story."

"Have you ever been hypnotized?" He asked.

I hadn't. So he hypnotized me—and it changed my life because I discovered that I was in denial. I was lying to myself and other people, and I didn't even *know* it.

To my surprise, when he put me into an altered state and asked me a question, the truth started to emerge. I thought, "I don't want to answer him this way. I'm going to find something else to tell him." But while I was thinking that, my mouth was telling him what was true. I loved it and I hated it. I was so impressed after working with him for a while that I launched my own hypnotherapy career in Santa Rosa, California.

About five or six years later, I had the awesome, coincidental pleasure of meeting Miguel Ruiz, the man who would later write *The Four Agreements*. I became his apprentice, and for ten years, I followed him around the world to pyramids and sacred sites in Mexico, Guatemala, Honduras, and Egypt—and into the inner worlds of the dreaming mind. It helped me to go even further, to see with clarity what my strategies for getting acceptance were, and how to break them.

My teaching, workshops, and hypnotherapy changed and segued, and a whole new world opened up to me—a whole new way of approaching love, life, and everything that any of us are concerned with. It's my brand of what he taught, combined with hypnotherapy and everything else I've ever done.

This book is called *THE NEW RELATIONSHIP: Reclaiming the Freedom to Love Without Fear*, because very few of us were shown what love without fear feels like. In the following chapters, I'll introduce you to five new "agreements" that have the power to transform the way you experience love in every relationship.

The thing I love about these agreements (or beliefs) is that each one of them confronts choices that we made when we were little—along with beliefs we were taught—and changes them.

When we release the programming responsible for the old choices we made based on beliefs, we become free to make new choices. We become free to be ourselves, exactly the way we are, and exactly the way we are not.

There are some really fundamental belief systems that were downloaded into us when we were too young to question them. Those belief systems were lies, and they are the reason we suffer in relationships. Now, that's not to blame the people who passed them on, because those beliefs had been downloaded into *their* minds when they were little. And so on, back through the generations—this heritage of downloaded lies.

My goal with this book is to help you break those beliefs and change them so your relationships become a source of joy and peace rather than suffering. While I'm going to direct a lot of my remarks towards romantic relationships, what I'm really talking about is *all* relationships, including and especially the relationship you have with yourself. If you don't have a viable, functional relationship with yourself, it's going to project itself out into the relationships you have with other people.

This book is about dreaming a new dream of relationship, both with others and with yourself. Each of the five agreements in this book is a doorway out of the nightmare and into what I call *The Dream of Heaven on Earth.*

The Dream of Heaven on Earth is a dream of truth, love, joy, peace, balance, acceptance, wisdom, creativity, patience, harmony, grace, gratitude, freedom, equality, and laughter. Once you know that it's possible to dream this dream, you'll also know that it's possible to live it.

One of the biggest lies you were taught is about the nature of love. In the next chapter, we'll unravel that lie, and you'll discover what love really is.

Let's begin.

Chapter 1
What is Love?

"How can it be love if it creates fear?"

— *Allan*

IT'S BEEN SAID THAT THE ESKIMOS OF THE FAR NORTH HAVE a very large number of words for snow and ice. It makes sense, since anyone living or working in a specialized environment would be likely to create a language that helps them communicate about their experiences.

Given that idea, have you noticed how few words we have in the English language for "love?" My thesaurus lists 13, including many love-lite words like "fondness" and "warmth." Is it possible that we do not have a large vocabulary of words for love because we do not live in an environment of love where we need a special language?

We use "love" for just about everything:

"I love your new hair color."

"I love chocolate chip cookie dough ice cream."

"I love you."

"I love to ski."

"I love it when you're nice to me."

"Do you love me?"

Some authors have attempted to differentiate qualities of love by adding Greek words to our daily language like "eros" and "agape," but I have never heard anyone speak them out loud.

So just what is this "love" thing? What are we talking about? Let's refine our understanding as a way to actually learn to love each other and ourselves more authentically.

I BELIEVE THAT WE ARE BORN AS LOVE

Imagine with me that there is a Creator of some sort, and that this Creator exists on the unmanifest side of the veil of creation—and we live on the manifest side. Let us also imagine that this Creator is Life itself, or the essence of unconditional love.

If that Creator wanted those of us on this side of the veil to have the experience of the pure love that exists on the unmanifest side, what better channel to create than a newborn baby?

You, born as one of those channels, came here to this manifest reality with no stories, no judgments or opinions, no politics, and no agenda about anything. As that infant, you were the embodiment of life without expectations.

Everyone wanted to pick you up, look you in the eye, and hold your eye contact for as long as possible. If you turned away, they tried to bring your attention back with all sorts of strange noises and facial contortions. They saw, unconsciously, that you were that channel of unconditional love, and they wanted to bask in your non-judgmental openness. They wanted to drink at your fountain of love.

So there you are, the channel for Creator's delight, pouring your unconditional acceptance into the world. And everybody is eating it up like starving souls at a free banquet. And you don't even know what you're doing because you don't know anything yet. You're just pure presence existing, being Life itself.

Unfortunately, this paradise cannot exist for very long. Like the story of Adam and Eve, the time comes when you must eat from the fruit of the tree of knowledge and learn about good and evil, right and wrong.

In the Toltec tradition, we call this process "domestication." It is the duty of your parents, and then society, to teach you the rules of their game. It is hard to teach you anything when you are basking in the glory of Your Divine Oneness, so they insist you make a new agreement with them. They require that you believe *they* are the source of love, not you.

You also agree that love is a commodity, you need it to survive, and it is somewhat scarce. Further, you agree to be good, and not bad, in order to receive your share of this commodity. You learn to be afraid that love will be withdrawn from you as punishment for being bad. This is the day that Adam and Eve left the Garden, and went forth and suffered, knowing their guilt and shame... and fearing God.

As the domestication continues, you make more and more agreements with parents, clergy, teachers, friends, Santa Claus, and God about what it means to be good and how to secure your share of the commodity of love and acceptance. You learn to domesticate yourself, to ensure that you will always win the approval of those who control the grades, the jobs, the romance, the money, the applause, and finally, the epitaphs.

If you are resonating with this, perhaps something different is stirring and awakening in you. Perhaps that something is your nature, your birthright as that pure channel of love that is still alive in you. I believe your nature is to pour that pure love into this manifest world.

I encourage you to remember this truth about yourself—that you are still that pure channel of love, and nothing has changed except your awareness of it.

THE LOVE THAT FLOWS THROUGH THAT CHANNEL IS PURE ACCEPTANCE

Without judgments or opinions or resistance to Creation, there is nothing left but the acceptance of what is. The love that is acceptance has no expectations or conditions. It needs nothing in return, and requires no response. You cannot bargain for this Love, and you also can never run out of it. The channel is connected to the Infinite Divine Source. That should be enough love for one lifetime!

So what is Love? I am suggesting to you that love is your nature, your birthright. And the love flowing out of you as acceptance of what is connects you with Life as the Divine Source, filling your heart with a joy and abundant happiness that can never be taken from you.

MATHEW AND ERICA: WHERE DID THE LOVE GO?

Mathew and Erica came to me because their marriage was in trouble. Mathew had confessed to a short affair, and Erica was devastated. She was very angry and said that at times she hated him. Mathew was lost in guilt and self-judgment, and in his resentment that Erica wouldn't forgive him.

Both partners believed they had been deeply in love before this incident, and now they could hardly look at each other. Erica wasn't sure she could forgive her husband, and his guilt was causing him to shut down and push her away. Their relationship had unraveled, and they could see no future for it.

Where did the love go?

As we explored the history of their six-year marriage, we revealed a pattern familiar to me. They had met and fallen in love almost instantly. Erica said they called themselves "soulmates" in the early months, and they both knew it would be a perfect relationship forever.

As time passed, little problems and hidden irritations arose, but they were both dedicated to keeping the love alive. They buried the red flags and decided to get married after six months.

Mathew and Erica told me they both expected the marriage vows and ceremony, along with the documents they signed, to hold them together and ensure they could ride over any rough spots that might come along.

They were surprised when I suggested the marriage license and vows were an agreement to become exclusive sources of the commodity of love, affection, and attention for each other. By taking his attention and affection outside the marriage, Mathew had broken the agreement. He had deprived Erica of her source of a commodity.

In my early meetings with Mathew and Erica, they learned how their childhood conditioning had taught them that love is a commodity they had to bargain for, earn, and do whatever was necessary to keep. They were surprised to acknowledge how much fear they had each been living in… the fear of losing the commodity of love they had been so happy to capture.

Where did the love go?

It turns out that the kind of love many relationships are based on is not really love at all. How can it be love if it creates fear? How can it be love if it can disappear and turn to anger, hate, and guilt so quickly?

Perhaps it isn't actually adult love at all, but an unmet need from childhood to earn approval, attention, acceptance, and safety. That need is projected into adult romantic relationships, along with the belief that we must perform to capture the commodity. There's a limited supply, we have to compete for it, and once we get it, we must hold onto it at any cost.

Real love is acceptance. When we accept someone just as they are, without bargains or expectations, we are truly loving them. When we accept *what is,* our hearts stay open to the truth of life's mysterious unfolding.

Where does love as acceptance go?

Nowhere.

This love is here, right in this moment, underneath the fear and doubt from your domestication. It is that infant in you, open and innocent. It *is* you. It is the I AM, that which is eternally present in all of Creation. Sure, go ahead and "love" your new car or your new romantic interest. And love Life. Love yourself—because you *are* Life, you *are* Love. Open the channel. Celebrate it. Celebrate you! Dance in joy with Life.

Your challenge: *Deny the lie that you are not good enough the way you are.* Embrace this new reality that you came here as Love, and you are still that same essence. You are a perfect expression of the life force that creates and animates this universe.

Anything else is a lie.

Chapter 2
A Modern Fairy Tale: How We Forgot That We Are Love

"You are the physical manifestation of the One Great Animator of Creation. There are no rules you need to follow, and no expectations you need to meet. You are here as a unique expression of that Divine Essence."

— *Allan*

ONCE UPON A TIME, IN A PLACE NOT SO FAR AWAY, THERE was born a little child. Perhaps it was you.

This little child was born into complete innocence and purity. It was a child of God and born as Love, like a gentle heart turned inside out—open, vulnerable, and pure.

The new Parents loved the child. But as time went on, the child began to express itself in the world. The Parents got angry at the child for crying and told it not to use that angry tone of voice with them. They laughed at its fear and told it not to make so much noise. The child began to be afraid of the Parents and the World. Most of all, this precious child of Love began to be afraid of its own feelings and sense of reality.

Now, totally unbeknownst to anyone, deep inside this little child were actually *two* children—a little girl and a little boy. You might think of them as the feminine and masculine energies that live inside each of us. The little girl part felt the feelings, needs, and sensitivities inside this special child. She is the one who felt so hurt when she was shamed, yelled at, or made wrong for being herself.

Right next to that inner little girl was the little boy. He hated to see her hurt and sad all the time, and he was angry at the Parents. So he spoke up and said: "NO, you are mean! Don't talk to us that way! Love us!"

The Parents had no tolerance for that kind of defiance. They showed the little boy part (masculine protector) how impotent he really was to protect the little girl part (feelings). He was just a child, after all, and the Parents ruled. Through their actions and words, whether subtle or not-so-subtle, the child learned that nobody would love it unless both the inner little girl and the inner little boy acted the way the Parents told them to. After all, the Parents knew the way the World expected them to act.

And so the little boy part turned to the little girl part inside, and said: "You have to be quiet! Don't cry, don't be hurt, don't show your fear, and don't tell the truth. You and your feelings are bad, and the Parents know it, and if you don't do all that stuff, maybe they will love us and not reject us and hurt our feelings so much. I'm not big enough or strong enough to protect us from Them, so we have to be quiet and do it their way."

The little girl part became silent, and she and the little boy part of our child of Love learned to look outside of themselves to see what was expected of them, what was allowed of them, and who they should be in order to be loved and accepted. Their survival depended on being loved and accepted, so they were very afraid of being rejected and not loved.

The child of Love died, and the child of Fear was born. The little boy part became the voice of the Parents and the World, making the little girl part wrong for being who she was. And thus was born the Inner Judge.

To this day, even now that the special child is all grown up, the little boy Judge within is still telling the little girl within to be quiet, to not express her feelings or her truth, and to do everything the way *They* say she should.

To make sure that she remembers, he reminds her constantly that she is not okay the way she is. She has to do it better, be more, be stronger and less emotional, and mostly be like *Them*—in order to have the love and acceptance she and he need to survive in the world.

What happened to that child of Love—that innocent being who once knew it was the source of love itself? In the pages that follow, we begin the journey of remembering.

Chapter 3
Your Personal Dream Shapes Every Relationship

"Until all humans understand that they are dreaming real-ity, and that each person's dream is the truth for them but no one else, only then will there be peace in the hearts of all humans, and the broken heart of the world can heal."

—*Allan Hardman*

WE LIVE IN A DREAM. NOT THE KIND YOU HAVE AT NIGHT, but a waking dream—a mental and emotional projection of reality, shaped by everything you've been taught, everything you've experienced, and everything you believe.

Perhaps you've heard this "dreaming" concept in different spiritual traditions. Whether this is the first time you're hearing about it, or you've encountered this teaching before, let me quickly clarify *exactly* what I mean by it, and how we can use the understanding of it to fall more deeply in love.

Right now, at this very moment, and in *every* moment of your life, you are not seeing what is "out there." The light you perceive reflects off the objects in the universe and enters your mind through your eyes, along with similar information collected by all of your senses. Together, they create a little virtual reality in your mind. The image you see is in your mind, not out there in the universe.

You cannot perceive your world any other way.

I remember a drawing in my school biology textbook of a tree and an eyeball. It illustrated that when you look at a tree, you are not really seeing the tree. It showed how light reflected off the tree passes through the lens of your eye, stimulates the rods and cones, and is transformed into neural impulses that travel into your brain and reproduce an image of the tree. Because of how the lens of your eye works, it actually projects the image of the tree upside down on the back of your eye. Your mind inverts the image.

Fascinating, isn't it? You are not really seeing what is out there in the world; you are looking at an inverted image made from reflected light and neurological impulses projected into your mind. You are looking at a little Virtual Reality that exists only in your mind.

And here's where it gets complicated: We think everyone else is seeing the virtual reality that *we're* seeing. We assume everyone lives in *our* dream—or that their dream *should* be like ours.

Imagine what the world looks, smells, and sounds like to a snake in the grass, a bat tracking a mosquito with its sonar, a worm tunneling through the garden soil, or an eagle soaring on an updraft. The quality and scope of the images collected and processed by their brains create a world in their minds that we would not recognize at all. What, then, is the real world? The worm's? The eagle's? Yours?

The Toltecs teach that each of us lives inside a *personal dream*. That personal dream is totally unique to you. You think you're seeing the world clearly, but you're really only seeing your interpretation—or dream—of the world. This illusion is the root of almost every misunderstanding, disappointment, and conflict in relationship.

WE DISTORT THE INFORMATION IN THE LIGHT

As the light, sound, and other perceptions are collected by our physical senses, they must travel through our *channels of perception* before they project the virtual reality in our minds. These channels are filled with what the Toltecs call "stored light," which consists of all of the experiences, memories, beliefs, and opinions collected throughout a lifetime.

As the incoming sensory information passes through these channels, it picks up pieces of stored light that are similar in quality, so that by the time it creates the virtual reality in the mind, it is very different from what the senses actually brought in from the outside world.

Very early in your life, you began collecting and storing knowledge about what is good and what is bad; who is right and who is wrong. You stored emotional memories and fears. Your parents, siblings, relatives, teachers, religious leaders, peers, magazines, and TV all downloaded information into your mind about the world, how it should be, and how you should be in it.

You stored opinions about sex, drugs, and rock and roll—not to mention politics, love, work, money, marriage, God, anger, and your body. That process has continued all of your life, supplemented by lovers, mates, bosses, talk show hosts, and beer commercials. All that knowledge is stored in your channels of perception, and it distorts the reality perceived by your senses.

The best way to describe this virtual reality is to call it a dream. We are all dreaming. This dreamed reality is unique and personal, and does not exist anywhere in the outside world.

Imagine that five people go to a party. The first is someone who has known and loved you since childhood. She meets a stranger and tells him about her long-time friend, you.

The next person to arrive is your mother, who meets the same stranger and tells him all about her wonderful (or incomprehensible) child.

Then someone who is angry with you arrives and shares yet another version of you. The fourth person to arrive at the party is an ex-lover of yours (you know the one) who has a big story of their own to share.

Finally, you arrive at the party. You meet the stranger and share your story about yourself. The stranger believes he has heard about five different people! He has heard five different dreams of you, each true for the teller.

Which story describes the real you? *Is* there a real you? What, then, is reality?

There is tremendous freedom in the awareness that you are dreaming. When you recognize that your dreamed reality is unique to you and you alone, you will no longer need to defend your point of view or convince anyone that they are wrong about theirs. You will honor your beliefs and opinions as absolutely true, but true for you only. You will respect the beliefs of every other person, knowing that how they dream is the perfect expression of who they are and from whence they have come.

This freedom is not easily won. The old dream is strong. It knows who is right and who is wrong, what is good and what is bad. You learned it long ago. It is embedded deeply in the recesses of your mind and shared by most of your culture.

Our lives are filled with examples of how believing that our personal dream is the truth creates conflict and separation. A mother alienates her teenage daughter in a fight about the family rules. A husband and wife grow distant from arguing over who is right about the best way to manage money. Your inner voices argue about which outfit to wear, the mistakes you make, and the best course of action in your business.

Religious organizations split over interpretations of doctrine. Saints are venerated and sinners are persecuted. Sides are chosen and conflict follows. Right and wrong circle each other, looking for weakness, proving points, creating winners and losers. The opinions, fears, and dogmas learned and believed create conflict, war, divorce, hurt, anger, hatred, and death.

If you believe that the personal dream in your mind is a true representation of what is "out there," it will cause you endless conflict and suffering. You will believe that you are right about what you see and know, and others are wrong. You will create conflict through your need to convince others and defend yourself. You will be afraid of being wrong.

There is a simple price for freedom from the conflict and difficulties that I have described above:

Understand that you are dreaming, and give up your need to be right.

The price is simple, but it is not easy. Your entire identity is created by, and depends on, what you believe is right. When you know you are right about politics and wars, global warming and the rainforest, teenage morality, the best spiritual path and the right diet, you feel safe. It is as though you have created a little island of safety in the midst of the chaos and turmoil of a confusing and unpredictable world.

The price of freedom is to leave that island of safety, to face the unknown, and to understand that you do not know, and perhaps will *never* know what is true and real in this universe. You can only dream your dream of it— and every other person can only dream their dream of it.

By leaving your island of safety, you will discover that the fears, opinions, and beliefs programmed into your mind are mostly lies that you were required to believe as a child.

CECILIA AND ROBERT: WHO'S RIGHT AND WHO'S WRONG?

Early on in my counseling practice, I worked with a young couple whose different personal dreams collided and created friction in their marriage. Cecilia and Robert had a pretty good relationship, but there was one thing they could never agree on.

Robert enjoyed watching sports on TV, and Cecilia thought it was a waste of time. She would often complain to Robert about it, and it was a big source of conflict in their marriage. Robert would say he needed the downtime to relax from work. Cecilia insisted he thought the sports were more important than her.

They argued about this issue more than they wanted to admit when we got together to talk about it. Both Cecilia and Robert believed they knew the **truth** about "TV sports," and no matter how much they argued, they could never convince the other that they were right and resolve the issue.

Robert had become very defensive about his TV sports, and Cecilia was growing increasingly hurt that he wouldn't listen to her reasoning and do what she wanted. They actually came to me each hoping I would "tame" the other and convince the other they were right. It didn't work—but, gratefully, something else did.

As I shared the concept of "dreaming" with Robert and Cecilia, they began to witness the ways they were distorting "TV sports" into totally different realities— ones that existed *only* in each of their minds. As an exercise, I sent them into the world to ask people about TV sports, and they were astounded to find that no two people had the same dream of its value, interest, worth, reaction, or meaning. Everyone had a unique way of interpreting what they perceived—and creating their own personal dream of it.

I call arguing about issues like this "Right/Wrong Ping Pong" because what we are saying in an argument is: "The way my mind interprets and distorts reality is right, and the way your mind distorts it is wrong! My reality is the *real* reality!" Since everyone knows they are right, nobody wants to be made wrong. And the only way to be right is to make the other person wrong. Back and forth, back and forth.

There are no winners in Right/Wrong Ping Pong. Everyone loses. Feelings are hurt, the fear of being wrong intensifies the fight to be right, and the ping pong goes on until someone pretends to give in, leaves the room angry, or simply learns to shut up and not bring up the issue.

Cecilia and Robert learned an amazing thing: They were both *right!* They were each describing their individual dreams, which were exactly right and true for each of them—and not for the other. They also learned they were both *wrong*, because the dream they were describing had nothing to do with any reality that actually existed outside of their minds.

From their perspective of increased awareness, these two learned to honor each other's dreams of reality. They learned to negotiate agreements about how those dreams could interface. Cecilia saw that Robert's desire to watch TV sports was not a personal rejection of her. And Robert learned to listen and respond to Cecilia's need for assurance and communication without having to stonewall her to protect his downtime.

Robert and Cecilia became winners of the We're Right/We're Wrong Silly Game of Life. Their communications became more real and more respectful, and they grew more curious about how the other was dreaming life. It became fun to be different.

How about you? Do you fight to be right by making someone else wrong? What would you lose if you couldn't be right? Until all humans understand they are dreaming reality, and that each person's dream is the truth for them but for no one else, only then will there be peace in the hearts of all humans, and the broken heart of the world can heal.

Remember, you are *dreaming!*

People are rarely interested in hearing that their opinions and beliefs are not "true" outside of their own minds. But I have faith in you and your ability to question what you know to be true. I have faith in your desire to transform your relationships by being willing to dream life from a new perspective.

When you are willing to accept this idea that you and your partner are dreaming uniquely different and perfect dreams of reality based on how each of you distorts the incoming light, you can be free to love and accept yourself and each other without resistance, judgment, blame, or fear. Without fear, your nature is to love. Fear closes your heart; love opens it. I want you to love with your heart wide open. And I believe *you* want that too.

Your challenge: *Surrender your need to be right.* If you understand that you and everyone else are dreaming a different dream of "reality," are you ready to accept that you are only right for yourself, and everyone else is right for themselves? This surrender will end conflict in all of your relationships.

THE NIGHTMARE IS BELIEVING THE DREAM IS REAL

When you forget that you are dreaming, the dream becomes a nightmare. Because now, you believe the distorted virtual realities in your mind, which include what others have taught you. Things like:

"I'm not good enough."

"Love is a commodity outside of me that must be earned."

"I'm responsible for other people's feelings."

"I need someone to complete me."

"I can't be myself and be loved."

You live by these agreements without realizing they are optional. You suffer. You blame others for your pain. And in relationship, you play out the same patterns over and over again because the dream keeps bringing you the same results, no matter what you intend.

Let's imagine you sit down at the keyboard of your mind, and you type in, "love, relationship, sex, happiness." You hit PRINT, and out comes the same old nightmare. So you read more books, attend more seminars, and learn new tools. You type in "love, relationship, sex, happiness" again—this time really carefully—and still, the same painful printout comes out. That's when you realize the problem isn't you, it's the *program.*

YOU ARE THE DREAMER

The good news is, you are no longer the vulnerable child who had to conform or perish. You are not the dream. You are the dreamer, and the dreamer can change the dream. This is where your freedom begins. When you become aware of your dream, you gain the power to transform it. You gain the power to wake up and become lucid in your own life. You begin to dream *consciously*.

It is never too late to have a rational adulthood. It is never too late to change your dream, to reprogram the lies downloaded into your mind, and create a life based on truth, presence, and true intimacy.

Someone told me recently that it sounded like a lot of work. My reply was: "Yes, it's true, it takes some effort, but think about how much effort it takes to obey rules that make no sense, to keep agreements that go against our very nature, and to justify and defend beliefs that were never ours in the first place."

The five new agreements that follow are tools to help you dream from love instead of fear.

Chapter 4
Five New Agreements to Make Love Come True

"All relationships are based on agreements, and in the Old Dream those agreements are mostly fear-based, unspoken, and unconscious."

— Allan

SOME TIME AGO, I WOKE UP BEFORE DAWN WITH FIVE NEW agreements about relationships in my head. I wrote them down and went back to sleep.

When I woke up later, I looked at them and thought, "That's interesting. Maybe I can do something with these." So I changed the order around, added some agreements, rewrote a few, and then deleted them again. In the end, the original five survived intact, exactly as they had been given to me in the middle of the night.

When I talk about agreements, I'm referring to the human capacity to choose and embrace beliefs as truth.

Many of the agreements we live by were made uncon-sciously when we were too little to understand what we were agreeing to. Imagine signing contracts as a three-year-old. That's essentially what we did.

Once you have this awareness, then you can ask your-self, "Do I choose to keep this agreement that I made when I was three years old that I've been honoring and keeping ever since? Does it make me happy? Does it contribute to my sense of well-being, self-love and worthiness in the world? Does it contribute to my ability to go into the world with my heart open and feel love for creation?"

If the old agreement doesn't do that, if it causes you to reject yourself or some part of yourself, then you get to say, "No, that does not make me happy. I want to change this agreement to something that makes me happy."

Here are five old agreements about relationships that so many of us made without knowing it:

1. Love is a commodity that lives outside of me, and I have to be good enough to earn it.
2. I'm responsible for the emotional reactions of others.
3. I am incomplete, and I need someone to complete me.
4. The outcomes of my relationships are more important than the truth of my feelings.

5. True happiness comes when I am the recipient of love.

In the chapters that follow, I'll share how we made these agreements and why they aren't true. I'll also invite you to consider five new agreements with the power to transform your relationships.

Let's begin with the biggest lie most of us were taught: Love is something outside of you.

Chapter 5
Agreement #1: Your Nature is Love. You Are the Source of Love in Your Life

"True happiness is the result of knowing yourself AS love."

— *Allan*

WHEN YOU WERE LITTLE, AS PART OF YOUR DOMESTICATION, you learned that love is something you have to earn, behave well for, bargain for, wait for, and be good enough to receive. Maybe, if you get it just right, someone will give it to you. That's "The Old Relationship." That's the dream we inherited. And it is a lie.

Even in the most loving families, this message gets passed on. No matter how well-intentioned our parents are, most of us unconsciously come to believe that we must be good to get our needs met and be worthy of love.

THE OLD DREAM: LOVE AS A COMMODITY

In the old dream that was drummed into us as children, love is a commodity—something scarce and vital that we need from others to survive. From the time we were babies, we learned that if we cried too much, they got annoyed. If we made them smile, they gave us attention. If we behaved, they loved us.

And when we're little, our survival depends on getting the approval, attention, and care from those around us. Anytime they're annoyed or impatient with us, or they don't come when we cry, on some level we understand: *I'm doing it wrong. I'm not meeting their needs. What do I have to do to meet their needs so they will meet my needs?*

We become little strategists, wearing masks and adopting roles to hook attention and approval. We become actors in a drama where survival means learning the rules of getting love from parents, teachers, lovers, even God.

In that dream, we believe that Love lives *out there*, and we need to *go get it*. We also believe we must modify ourselves to be lovable.

When we fall in love, it feels magical. But underneath that magic is an unspoken transaction. "You give me attention, I give you affection. You give me security, I give you sex. You love me, and I'll stay lovable for you."

Until someone breaks the rules. Looks at the waitress. Stops calling. Forgets to say, "I love you." Then we panic, because they were our source of love, and our source just wandered off.

THE FEAR OF BEING LEFT OUT, ALONE, OR UNLOVED

When our childhood experiences created fear because our parents weren't able to be present for us—perhaps because of alcohol, affairs, work, divorce, health issues, or their own wounding—those fears live on in our inner child and affect how we choose our adult love relationships. These actions and reactions are mostly subconscious and need to be gently invited into our adult awareness so we can address them.

Almost all children blame themselves when their needs are not met or when something goes wrong in the family. When parents divorce, get sick, suffer from migraines, lose someone, or simply ignore or over-punish them, the child thinks it's their fault. If *they* could have been better behaved, quieter, or more perfect, everything would be okay.

If your childhood was difficult in any way (and almost all are), there may be a little part of you—your inner child—who is afraid they failed to earn the commodity of love because of defects or failures. That child will create relationships in your adult life based on the fear of not being good enough for the commodity of love, and being afraid of losing it once it is found.

You will know you are being controlled by your inner child in your relationships if you feel fear. If you worry about getting it right for your partner, if you sacrifice your needs to take care of others, if you are haunted by fears that your partner is interested in someone else—these are signs that your childhood fears are leaking into your adult relationships.

Your relationship may have been shaped by the fears of your inner child (or your partner's), but that doesn't make it wrong or broken. Becoming aware of these hidden forces in how relationships form and operate is not a reason for alarm—or for running off into the sunset. Take gentle time to acknowledge these possibilities, bring love to them, and keep going. The most important thing is to be gentle with yourself and others.

YOU ARE THE SOURCE OF LOVE IN YOUR LIFE

Love has never been outside of you. It *is* you. But when you became old enough to understand, they started to train it out of you. They taught you how to behave to be loved and how to abandon your truth to fit the dream. You stopped crying when you needed to cry. You smiled when you didn't feel like smiling. You held in your needs, your feelings, and your anger. You learned that love came from *them*, and the price of that love was your authenticity.

The New Relationship starts with a new agreement: **"I am the source of Love."** This changes the whole dynamic. Instead of scanning the room for someone to hook, someone to impress, someone to fill the hole inside you… you show up fully, radiating and over-flowing.

Instead of asking: "How can I hook love today?"

You ask: "Where can I share my love today?"

That's the transformation. Instead of a cup waiting to be filled, you are the ocean, offering the world a sip.

EYE CONTACT IS A HOLE IN THE MASK

One of my favorite things is what happens when you make eye contact with an infant. They're seeing you *without judgment*, and that's thrilling! It's thrilling because eye contact is a hole in the mask, and for a moment, we see ourselves reflected back without all the judgments. We remember who we are.

But eye contact is also terrifying, because once we're domesticated, we become afraid of allowing people to look us in the eyes and see through the hole in the mask. We know that we're not lovable the way we are because our parents rejected us for being ourselves. We worry that someone else will see what they saw and reject us, too. This is why it's so difficult to maintain eye contact for longer than two seconds—because we are afraid of being seen.

If we enter romantic relationships trying to gain approval and love by being what our partner wants us to be, we are doomed. It will not be a conscious relationship; it will be a dance of lies. You deserve better. If you are pretending to be someone you aren't to hold on to a relationship, you have already lost it. And, most importantly, you have lost your relationship with yourself.

Love is not a commodity that lives outside us. Love is everywhere! The moon loves us. The sun loves us. The air loves us. Take a deep breath right now... a deep, conscious breath. The air that you breathe loves you. It gives and sustains your very Life itself. That is love. Breathe again. Deeply and gently receive the gift of love.

The moon and sun and air don't demand anything from you to love you and give you the gift of Life. There are no bargains needed, no commitments to make, and no obligations created when you accept that love. It is freely given, and freely received.

Your challenge: Embrace knowing that you are the source of love in your life.

1. **Remember the Truth.** Know that love flows through you as Life itself, as the Divine nature that is in and through all of Creation. There is nowhere in Creation that this Divine Force is not present. It is in and through you. It is your nature. It is now, and has always been what you are.

2. **Share Your Love.** Today, instead of going into your world looking for sources of love, attention, or appreciation, try going out there wondering where you can share your love. Love doesn't run out. Be generous with it. Let it be your offering to the world, simply because it's who you are. How many ways can you say, "I love you" to all of Creation today?

3. **Be Gentle With Yourself.** You've spent decades playing by the old rules. Be patient. Laugh when you fall back into the old dream and come back to the truth.

You don't need to be different. You don't need to be "better." You are already Love. That's the good news. That's the *best* news. When you stop believing you're empty, you stop grasping. When you stop grasping, you stop suffering. And when you stop suffering, your love becomes a gift instead of a transaction.

Chapter 6
Agreement #2: You Are Not Responsible for the Emotional Reactions of Others (to Your Reality)

"They're not responding to you—they're responding to their dream of you. And that dream has nothing to do with you."

—Allan

LET'S GO SLOW WITH THIS ONE, BECAUSE IT MIGHT RATTLE some old wiring.

We came into this world as Life itself. We had no opinions, no knowledge, and no fear. We had virtually nothing. And then people started hooking our attention and telling us when we were good, bad, right, and wrong.

As we got older and started being physical, we broke things, we spilled things, we fell down and skinned our knee when they told us not to run. They started telling us, "I'm so angry, I'm so hurt because of what you did. Why can't you be more careful? Why aren't you paying attention?"

Imagine a little four-year-old trying to answer. As that child, we know we don't want Mom to be angry because she could abandon, leave, or punish us. So we have to figure out what this "paying attention" thing is so we don't make her angry.

The tendency in us as kids is to start pulling in our arms, our enthusiasm, and our lifeforce to "be careful and pay attention." And every time somebody says, "Watch out!" the attention goes to the person yelling, and not to what we're doing. Then we fall and cut ourselves, and they say, "See? God, you frustrate me."

I spend a lot of time in villages in Mexico where six-year-old kids have machetes—knives that would make a modern mother in the U.S. faint—and they're taking the ends off of coconuts and swinging them hard. They know where their hand is, they know where the coconut is, and they know where the machete goes. Nobody is yelling, "Be careful! Why aren't you paying attention?" You can't be looking over your shoulder to see who's yelling at you when you're swinging a two-foot machete at a coconut! These kids don't have to "be careful." They already know they don't want to hit their hand with a machete.

In all the time I've been living in Mexico, I've seen very few people with missing fingers from childhood. Just like we've seen very few kids with their eyes poked out from running with a stick.

And when you get good grades? "You make me so proud." Or company is over, and mom says, "Come on out here. Show everybody how you dance to the music!" And as a child, you don't want to, so you say, "No, I don't want to," and then mom is embarrassed. So she says, "You make me angry. You get out here and do this!" So maybe you get out there and do what you're supposed to do, and then later she says, "Thank you, you make me so proud when... blah, blah, blah."

And so we learn that we're responsible for other people's emotional reactions. We learn that whatever we're doing is what causes them to be happy or distressed. And if they're distressed, they don't meet our needs. So we have to figure out what we're doing wrong so they don't get distressed or angry at us. We start becoming more and more vigilant about how people react to us.

Sadly, the more difficult our parents are, the more stress they have, and the more poison they're carrying emotionally—the more deeply we learn that we have to manipulate our reality to manage and manipulate *their* emotional responses, so we can get our needs met.

Most of us were taught that it is bad to hurt other people's feelings, to be selfish by taking the last cookie, or to act in ways that make people angry. You learned to bargain away your integrity and emotional truth to protect the feelings of others. You agreed to create responses in them that assured you that you were worthy of receiving your share of the commodity of love. It became your job to manage the moods and reactions of others.

Be quiet so Mom doesn't get mad.

Be cheerful so Dad doesn't leave.

Don't cry; it upsets them.

Be good and don't make waves.

We carried that behavior into adulthood. So now, when someone is upset, we panic: *What did I do? How can I fix this?* We jump into guilt, shame, blame, or defensiveness. We learned that if someone's upset, *I'm the reason.*

That was a lie—a very old, very convincing lie. And now we're breaking it.

THE DREAM OF THE WORLD

The truth is, you are not responsible for causing anyone's emotional reaction. You never have been.

Whatever is real for you is not why other people get upset. What's true for you—what you do, what you say, how you act—is *not* what causes other people to have their emotional reactions.

The guilt, the tiptoeing, the second-guessing, the people-pleasing, the desperate attempts to manage how others feel about you—none of it is your job. You didn't cause their emotional response, and you *can't*. You are not *capable* of creating emotional reactions in other people, because everyone's emotional reactions arise from their interpretations and assumptions, not directly from the actions of others.

You cannot create emotional reactions in others, and they cannot create emotional reactions in you. As we've already covered, each of us lives in a *virtual reality*—a dream created in our minds.

Everything we perceive passes through our own channels of perception, and those channels are clogged with trauma, fear, opinions, religion, and memory. So when you look at someone, you're not seeing *them*, you're seeing the dream version of them crafted in your own mind, distorted by your past and colored by your beliefs. When someone looks at *you*, they're seeing the *dream version* of you crafted in *their* mind, distorted by their past, and colored by their beliefs.

You're not reacting to each other. You're reacting to your *stories* about each other. You react to another person based on *the story you're telling yourself* about their words or actions. They react to you based on the story they're telling themselves about your words and actions.

This is extraordinarily profound and freeing, because if it's not true that we're directly causing other people's emotional reactions to us, we can quit worrying about it. We can quit manipulating *our* reality to manipulate *their* reality to make them feel the way we think they should, so they'll treat us the way we want to be treated.

Years ago, after one of my teaching circles, I received two messages. The first one said, "That was the best circle you've ever led. I was blown away. I hope you teach them like this in the future." The second one said,

"That was the worst circle I've ever been to. If you lead like that again, I'm out."

Same event, two completely opposite emotional reactions. That's when I really saw that people are dreaming their own dream of you. They'll praise you or criticize you based on *that dream*, not who you really are. And if you react to those dreams—if you try to manage them—you become a puppet on strings. Their approval lifts you up, and their disapproval tears you down. But when you know you're not responsible for other people's emotional reactions, nobody gets to pull your strings. Not even your mother. Not even your partner. Not even the judge inside your own head.

I prefer to be free from being a puppet. People can say, "You're great." "You're not great." "You're the best." "You're the worst." "You're ugly." "You're buff." And I get to be free from my up-and-down emotional reactions to that.

SAME EVENT, DIFFERENT STORY

Let's say you're downtown and you see your girlfriend or boyfriend walking ahead of you on the sidewalk holding hands with somebody else, and you have an emotional reaction. Maybe you're hurt, angry, or afraid. You might run home and crawl under the covers, or you might scream and run up behind them, ready for a fight.

But let's look at the very same scenario, and *this* time, imagine that you've been seeing someone else. Maybe you haven't told your boyfriend or girlfriend about your new relationship because you were afraid of their emotional reaction, and because you believed you were going to hurt them. Now you see them walking down the street with someone else, and you're elated. It's the exact same event, but a totally different reaction depending on how you're dreaming it.

If more than one reaction is possible, how can we say that the event or the words cause our emotional reaction? We can't. We have to tell a story about it first.

THE EMOTIONAL EQUATION

Here's a simple tool you can use to determine what's actually causing your emotional reaction:

Draw three columns on a page.

• **Column 1: Event** — what actually happened.

• **Column 2: Story** — leave this blank at first.

• **Column 3: Emotion** — what you felt.

Fill in Column 1 and Column 3 first. For example, in Column 1 you might write, "I saw my partner holding hands with someone else," to describe the event. In Column 3, you might write, "sad, angry, and heartbroken," to name the emotions that arose.

Most people think the event caused the emotion. But there's *always* a story in between. Now, in Column 2, write down the story you told yourself about the event. What story created the fear, the anger, the jealousy, the feeling of powerlessness? Perhaps it was, "This always happens to me." Or maybe it was, "Now I'm going to be alone forever."

Now examine the story. Is it actually the truth? If the story you're telling creates fear, anger, or powerlessness, it's not the truth; it's just a story.

The event is not doing this to you. The universe is not making you sad. The universe is not making you angry. It doesn't have the power to do that. The Universe is just here.

Whether it's a beautiful, starry night, or some part of the universe that backs into your car in the parking lot, there's no emotional content to it whatsoever. Outside the human mind, a car backing into another car contains no emotion, because there's no story anywhere but in the human mind.

It's *never* the event that causes the emotional reaction. It's *always* the story.

After teaching about this, someone once asked me, "So are you saying that if I punch someone in the face, I'm not responsible for causing their emotional reaction???"

You're responsible for creating the event, but not the emotional reaction. If you physically hurt somebody, the story they tell about it is what creates their emotional reaction. You can certainly be responsible for what that action creates in *your* life. But you are not responsible for the emotional reaction they have to being punched in the nose. They could be angry. They could be sad. They could be humiliated. They could be delighted. All of those emotional reactions are already in their body waiting for a story to trigger the matching one.

Picture this: You're in a bar. A big guy growls, "You lookin' at me?" You walk over and punch him in the nose. He's ecstatic! He finally gets to pour all his stored poison out on somebody. And now it's pouring out… onto *your* nose.

Or… same punch, different guy—who collapses in a corner, whimpering, "Why does everyone always hurt me?"

Same event. Two entirely different emotional reactions. The event didn't cause it. The interpretation did.

If you're the one feeling the impulse to go punch some-body—maybe he's being rude, being loud, saying disgusting things to women—pause before you act and notice the story you're telling. Are you becoming Sir Galahad rescuing the damsel, replaying a childhood drama of trying to protect your mother from your father?

It's all stories. The magic is in seeing them.

We can clear the stories out of our channels of percep-tion through meditation and through the column exer-cise I gave you. We reveal the old stories, we clean them out, and create new ones. Sometimes the new story is very simple and opens your heart instantly.

Occasionally I would be driving on the freeway, and a driver would cut me off. It would scare me and I'd be angry. I'd have a lot of judgments, and I'd tailgate them to show them how dangerous they were. I'd drive up next to them and stare at them with that look—you know the look! Suddenly I'd realize my body was flooded with emotional poison because of a story I told myself about what this person did.

So I changed the story. I imagined that a loved one was lying in the back seat of the car having a baby, and they were rushing to the hospital. So I'd back off right away and say, "God bless you both. Be careful! I'm out of your way. Go for it. I love you. Everything is going to be great." And suddenly, I'd be filled with love and happiness.

The story I tell myself about this incident is my choice. It has nothing to do with them cutting me off. They didn't even cut me off. That's the beginning of my story. In reality, they just changed lanes.

Event: Someone cut me off in traffic.

Story: They're endangering everyone on the road!

Emotion: Anger, rage.

New Story: Someone is in the back seat just trying to make it to the hospital. Or maybe they just need to get to a bathroom ASAP. I get it, buddy. Good luck!

New Emotions: Empathy, peace.

An old apprentice of mine heard this once, and she decided to take it even farther. She had a long commute to work every day on the freeway, and she said "I love you" to everybody in every car. She would look over at the driver and say, "I love you!" And if there were too many cars and she was going too fast, she said, "I love you! I love you! I love you!" rapidly.

Every time her mind wandered and she thought she would turn on the radio, she just came back to her spiritual practice. "I love you, I love you, I love you." By the time she got to work, she was in bliss. Before, she arrived at work saying, "Oh, my God, I barely survived. The roads are full of idiots. I hate them all." She just changed her story about it and was in love.

THE COROLLARY

There's a corollary to this new agreement that you are not responsible for the reactions of others to your reality, and it's this:

You *are* responsible for *your* emotional reactions to other people's reality, because now you know that you are the one creating your emotions based on how you dream.

That's the good news and the bad news. Maybe someone backs into your car. You now know that the event itself doesn't create the anger. The story you tell yourself about the event creates the anger. And you can change the story. You can change the story because anger is a waste of your precious life force.

I would rather be happy. I would rather have my heart open, so I choose a story that allows that. For me, the simplest, most powerful story is this:

This universe is perfect.

Everything is unfolding through cause and effect. If I hadn't parked in that spot, there would be no dent. If they hadn't been delayed by five minutes this morning, there would be no dent. If I hadn't been wandering around in the market, there would be no dent. So where is the villain here? No one "did" anything "to" me. I am not a victim. The universe simply moved two physical objects together in space and time.

So I put this into my chart:

Event: They backed into my car.

Story: Perfect universe.

Reaction: Peace. Equanimity. Openness.

With that story, my heart stays open to the other person, who is now scared and upset. "Oh my God, I hit your car!" From openness, I can respond with kindness. "Well… that must feel awful. It's okay." I don't add more trauma to their trauma. I stay in love.

We don't have to take care of other people's feelings to be okay. We don't have to feel guilty if someone says we "hurt" them. We don't have to get defensive if someone is angry with us because we know the truth: *We did not cause their emotional response.* They are reacting to the story **in their own dream.** They are interpreting. They are personalizing and distorting. They are describing their dream to us. They might be wagging a finger in our face, shouting, turning red… and we can simply watch, stay in our own center, and silently observe.

We don't have to enter their dream. We can keep our heart open and stay in love even as they spin in their own story.

WHATEVER YOU DO, DON'T GO AGAINST YOURSELF

You might be familiar with Miguel Ruiz's book, *The Four Agreements.* The first agreement is: Be Impeccable With Your Word. Almost everyone misunderstands it. They think it means always tell the truth and always keep your commitments. Nothing could be further from what Miguel meant. He defines "impeccable" from the Latin *impeccatus*—without sin.

And then he defines sin: sin is going against yourself, and using your word in a way that harms you. And the word is not just what you say. In fact, it's actually very little of what you say. Your word is all of the voices talking to you in your own head. Your word is the belief systems that are hidden from you in your subconscious mind, below your awareness, that are operating in your life. Your word is all the agreements you've made that manifest themselves as your actions and as what you say. So we can say that your word is your thoughts, your actions, your deeds, and your unspoken words.

To not use the word against yourself is to never judge yourself, because everything the inner judge says is a lie. To lie to yourself is to use your word against yourself. To be impeccable is to stay true to yourself instead of acting against yourself.

If you punch someone in a bar, you're likely acting against yourself, because the consequences of that punch probably won't be good for you. When we bring this understanding into responsibility for emotions, we suddenly have a guiding standard. We don't get to say, "I'm not responsible for your reaction to me," and then go around killing and pillaging. That's the immature misunderstanding.

To be impeccable means: I will not go against myself in order to manage your feelings. And here's the key— only *you* can know what "going against yourself" means for *you*.

Impeccability is self-defined and ever-evolving. We try something, and ten minutes later we might realize we've gone against ourselves. So we shift without judgment, because judging ourselves is also going against ourselves.

So let's pull the pieces together:

We are not responsible for causing other people's emotional reactions to us. We *are* responsible for our emotional reactions to other people's reality—to events in the world, to politics, to wars, to dented fenders, to babies dying of AIDS and starvation in Africa. None of these events carry emotional content of their own. We add that.

With awareness, we have choice about what emotional content we add—or don't add. By clearing out the stored light in our channels of perception, our awareness gives us the choice to change the stories we tell. Changing the stories changes the emotional reaction.

When we change the stories, we stop saying: "You hurt me." That's the old dream. In the old dream, we say, "You hurt me, and now I will forgive you," or we grovel and say, "I'm sorry, I must be bad—please forgive me."

That's the Judge and the Victim playing ping pong. Instead, we can say, "I forgive myself for using others to hurt myself." We can say, "I forgive myself for dreaming that they caused my emotional reaction." Because if I judge myself for that misunderstanding, I'm just going against myself again.

Being impeccable means you *don't go against yourself*. You live in integrity. You act with love. You follow your truth. And you also stop carrying emotional responsibility for other people's dreams.

YOU'RE FREE (AND SO ARE THEY)

When you realize that you're not responsible for other people's emotions, you get your freedom back. You stop performing, apologizing for your truth, and editing yourself to manage someone else's internal state. You just show up as you, and you let others dream you however they need to. That doesn't mean you go around being cruel or unkind. You don't get to say, "I'm not responsible for your feelings" while using your words like weapons. That would be going against yourself.

In The New Relationship, partners are free to be who they are and feel what they feel, and they respect each other's capacity to honor and embrace their own emotions. They do not manipulate their integrity in the name of taking care of their beloved.

In the next chapter, we'll look at what happens when you no longer depend on another person to feel complete, and begin to discover that wholeness does not come from relationship at all.

Chapter 7
Agreement #3: You Are Whole and Complete within Yourself

"Ultimately, relationship is not about two people interacting; it is the dance of love recognizing itself."

— Allan

So many of us were raised with the idea that somewhere out there is a person who will complete us. Our "other half." The missing piece that will finally make us whole.

It's a beautiful fantasy, but it's not the truth. The truth is that **you are already whole.** You came into this life complete, and you never needed someone else to complete you. The old belief that we're incomplete without a partner is just another dream we inherited from our childhood programming.

So we go looking—not for partnership, but for completion.

I used to be in the wedding business and provided a beautiful garden for people to get married in. During the wedding ceremony, the bride and groom would have two candles—one for her and one for him. They'd use them to light one candle, and then they'd both blow out their candle. "Now we are One," they'd say. My reaction was, "And you've just blown out your own light." The whole ceremony gave me cold chills.

MUTUALLY COMPATIBLE PATHOLOGIES

We see the same dream in singles ads and dating profiles. People list all the wonderful things they think they like to do and would want to do with a compatible partner:

I enjoy good movies, and...

Walks on the beach.

Fine dining.

Adventure.

Funny cartoons.

Slow dancing.

Romantic candlelit evenings.

Yoga.

Museums.

People may or may not actually do these things, but the desire is there. The trouble is that most relationships are not created based on lists of mutually compatible activities and interests. They're often created from projections, the unmet needs and emotional wounds of childhood, or the fear of being left out, alone, and unloved.

WHY OPPOSITES ATTRACT

We've all heard the saying that opposites attract. There's a reason for this!

When you were a young child, you learned how to earn love and acceptance in order to survive. If you were criticized for being lazy, you might have become very industrious. If you were shamed for being messy, you may have adapted by becoming exceedingly neat. If your feelings were rejected, perhaps you learned to deny them and to be very intellectual and thoughtful.

In order to become what your caregivers wanted you to be, you had to push these disowned parts of yourself into what psychologists call **the shadow**. Anything we learn to judge and reject about ourselves goes into our shadow.

Your soul longs for a reunion of these rejected parts of yourself, and will search the world for them in the hope of wholeness. Finding those lost parts of the self in another person can feel familiar and thrilling. If the other person also recognizes their split-off parts in you,

you may be powerfully attracted to each other as an instant remedy for the emptiness within.

This is what I call mutually compatible pathologies. Two people, each disowning opposite parts of themselves, come together and feel like one complete soul. It feels like fate, like love at first sight. What they're really falling in love with is themselves—their disowned parts projected onto the other person.

Let me tell you a little fairy tale to illustrate what I mean.

LOVE ACROSS A CROWDED ROOM

Once upon a time, in a place not so far away, there was a baby girl named Patricia. Her father was an engineer, and her mother was a professor at a local university. They believed in the power of logic, serious planning, and above all, being grounded and rational. They believed that only by using their minds and developing their intellect could they get what they needed from life, and they saw this as the reason they were successful.

Patricia came bounding into the world as all infants do —proclaiming, "I'm here! I am love itself!" Her parents quite naturally domesticated her into their dream by suggesting she tone down her energy and stop being so frivolous. When she was thoughtful and articulate, she was praised. When she was silly, wild, or too emotional, she got the message that it was "a little too much."

Patricia learned that her mind was her greatest asset, and unconsciously decided to deny the part of herself they labeled "childish" and push it into her shadow.

Meanwhile, there was a young boy named Jason, born into a very spiritual, easy-going family. He was taught by his parents to "live for today" and that everything would take care of itself.

Jason was encouraged to go into the arts and learned to play several instruments when he was young. He grew up painting, playing music, and building with his hands.

As he matured, he became an artist and, in order to make a living, became a carpenter, well known for his custom woodwork and attention to detail. He was fun to be around, very relaxed with long hair and faded jeans. He was loose and light, and people loved him.

If Jason ever asked, "Mom, what do I need to do to prepare for the future?" his mom would say, "Don't worry about all that. You'll be guided. Just live in the present and everything will be okay." So he buried his planning mind, suppressed his desire for order, and leaned even more into flow and chaos. His thoughtful, grounded, plan-for-the-future self went into his shadow.

Our story moves forward in time to when Patricia and Jason are in their mid-20s and at a party. Patricia has been invited by a friend who tells her she works too much, is too serious, and needs to get out more. She has a very good job at a publishing company, and she's rising fast in the business. Someone who knows Jason invites him too.

They're on opposite ends of the room and notice each other. Patricia likes Jason's relaxed appearance and long hair, and he finds himself attracted to how put-together and professional she appears.

He thinks, "Wow, that's not the kind of person I should be attracted to."

She wonders, "Who is that casual-looking guy? Everyone seems to like him, and the people around him are all laughing."

The evening progresses, Jason and Patricia end up talking, and before the night is over, he has her phone number. He calls her the next morning and they go out to lunch. The chemistry is so strong.

Patricia goes back to work and says to her colleagues, "You won't believe this guy—he's funny, he's relaxed, and he talks about the most amazing things. He's an incredible artist!"

Jason goes out with his friends and says, "I met this woman and she's really something. Not the type I thought I'd be attracted to—she works in publishing, wears nylons and heels—and she has her life really planned out. She knows what she wants and where she's going. That's so attractive to me!"

Pretty soon they're having lunch, dinner, lunch, dinner, and then breakfast. A couple of months later they move in together. Their chemistry is delicious and they can't get enough of each other. They tell their friends, "I've found my soulmate."

Patricia says, "He's adorable, he doesn't worry about anything, and he's really spontaneous and fun."

Jason says, "She's so grounded and organized. She keeps everything together."

About three months go by like this, and one morning she's getting up to go to work and he's just lying in bed. She's rushing around to get dressed and he's not worried about getting out of the house at all. For the first time, this irritates her.

She used to think it was so cute—"You're so sexy lying there when I go to work." But this time she looks at him and says, "Why aren't you getting up? Don't you have any plans? Being an artist is great, but you'll never amount to anything if you don't get serious."

Before he can think, he reacts: "You know, it would be great if you weren't so rigid and uptight all the time. You always have to rush off. You're always working."

Oops. They don't have time to talk about it because she's late for work, and she leaves.

Later, they make up because they don't want to lose the wonderful, boundless love they've been feeling, so they ignore the judgments that are beginning to crop up about each other. But the judgments don't go away.

Eventually they begin to argue more and more, until he moves out and they break up.

Jason, being the free spirit that he is, doesn't mind all that much and is soon open to the next person who comes along and wants to play. Patricia throws herself back into her work and judges him for being lazy and immature. She's relieved to be rid of him... and still, she keeps finding herself attracted to men just like him.

Why?

Way back at the beginning, when Patricia was told not to be frivolous, not to be joyous, not to be in the moment, but to plan for the future, she had to take the free-spirit part of herself and push it into her shadow. It still lives there, longing to come back into wholeness. She doesn't remember that this part of herself even exists. If it does show up, she thinks it's bad and pushes it away again.

Meanwhile, Jason has done the same thing with his intellectual, thoughtful, grounded side. His soul is longing for reunion with that part of himself, but he doesn't know that. If it does come up, he pushes it away.

These two people are going through life wanting wholeness, but they don't realize that the wholeness is already within them. They recognize their disowned parts "out there" in another person. They rush to each other, and their mutually opposite disowned parts make them feel like one complete soul. It feels like destiny. It feels like love. But it's really two shadows dancing.

Sooner or later, they begin to judge in the other person the very qualities that first drew them in. Confusion, doubt, and guilt take over.

MEET YOUR DISOWNED SELF

How can you figure out which aspects of yourself you have disowned, pushed into your shadow, and then projected onto others? It is very simple.

Ask yourself this question: **What annoys me the most (top ten!) about others?** And write down the answers you receive.

Here's one example.

Perhaps your husband is late all the time, and you're always on time. Your mind screams, "Irresponsible! Disrespectful!" You are always waiting for him to get ready, and he seems to have no sense of urgency.

This is a situation in which you have disowned the part of you that would like to relax sometimes and not always show up on time. Does this part of you really exist? Sure.

I believe that we are all whole. The entire range of human possibility dwells within each one of us. There-fore, even if you wouldn't be caught dead arriving late, and you judge others who do, that doesn't mean you can't appreciate the *possibility* of being late.

The only difference between you and those who are late is that you don't have permission to be late in your dreaming mind. Long ago, you were shamed or punished for it, or you were given subtle signals that being late isn't okay. You embraced that rule, and once we embrace a rule as "right," we expect everyone to abide by it.

Every time someone annoys you with a certain kind of behavior, you become annoyed because you judge that behavior. You learned to judge it because someone told you, usually when you were little, that it was bad or wrong. You took that potential in *yourself* and buried it, pushing it into your shadow. When it shows up in someone else, you judge it.

As a result, you don't have permission in your inner world to be late, take the last piece of cake, make a mistake, laugh loudly, cry, or do whatever it is that you judge. But that doesn't mean those potentials aren't in you. They're just hiding in the basement, waiting.

HOW TO BRING YOURSELF BACK INTO WHOLENESS

How can you free yourself of the annoyance you feel with a partner? The answer is simple, but not always easy:

Give yourself permission to accept in yourself the behavior, attitude, or beliefs that you judge.

That doesn't mean you have to start showing up late. But you *can* embrace the lateness that was always within you, that you disowned, and call it back home.

Just imagine it for a moment. Imagine the luxury of being late, taking your time, making sure your needs are met, and moving slowly to work. Wouldn't that feel kind of good? I'm not asking you to turn your life upside down. I'm asking you to open your heart to a part of yourself you've exiled.

Reclaiming these split-off parts doesn't mean you need to become them. It simply means you stop rejecting them and splitting them off. When we split them off, we're splitting off our energy, our aliveness, and beautiful, valuable parts of who we are. And it takes *a lot* of energy to keep pushing them away.

It's like sending a kid to their room, but they keep running down the hall, and you keep saying, "Get back to your room!" It's exhausting.

It's so much sweeter to embrace the totality of who you are. When you've come to acceptance and love for all parts of you, and you're not judging them, you're no longer searching for them "out there" and judging them in other people. Your heart is now open to every kind of person imaginable. They can be tidy when you're messy. They can be messy when you're tidy. They can be late when you're always on time.

The teacher Jesus once said something like, "Everything

that I am, you are. Everything you are, I am—or have been."

We're all late, we're all early, we're all tidy, we're all messy. But because of the domestication we went through when we were little, we showed up with what was accepted, and rejected in ourselves what was rejected out there. Unfortunately, when we left home, nobody said, "Hey, you don't have to worry about all that. Here are all your parts back. Have a nice life."

The parts of us that have been disowned are like orphaned children. Imagine walking into an orphanage and seeing all the kids acting out. One by one, you say, "Come here. Let me get to know you. Let me learn to love you. I won't keep projecting my judgment of you onto the world."

Another way to say it is this: everybody you judge or feel irritated by gets to be something you don't get to be. And your soul is longing to have that accessible. So anyone you judge out there, for any reason, is doing something you want to do—but you've told yourself you're not allowed to.

To embrace that part of yourself, you say, "Okay… let's talk. What do you want?" Maybe that part says, "I'm tired of rushing. I want to breathe. I want to loosen the grip a little."

You can negotiate. You don't have to abandon being conscientious. You don't have to become chronically late. But maybe you don't have to live in fear either—

the fear of being bad, losing approval, or not being loved.

That's the secret key to reclaiming the disowned parts of yourself. From there, you can begin loving them: *Come on home. Come back to the family. Let's fall in love. Let's be whole inside.*

THE INNER CHILD THAT QUIETLY SHAPES YOUR RELATIONSHIPS

It is often a surprise to people when I suggest it may be a child part within who is choosing and managing their relationships, especially their romantic ones.

I have supported countless couples sorting out issues in their relationships, and we very often discover they are reacting to wounds or using agreements they learned as children to manage their adult relationships.

Donna and Ben are a good example.

They had been married for three years when they contacted me. Their marriage was generally satisfying, but they were arguing about schedules. Ben finished work and was home for dinner before Donna, so he often prepared dinner. Donna often arrived home later than she planned, and Ben would be angry that "dinner was ruined" or that she just didn't appreciate what he was doing. Donna said Ben was "unrealistic" and should just relax about it.

After sharing these present-day issues, I encouraged them to look into the past.

We discovered Ben had been raised by a mother who constantly told him she would take him to soccer practice or a friend's house "in a minute" and left him waiting in the car while she talked on the phone until the practice was over or it was too late to play. It was a huge trauma for him, and the wound from the neglect of his childhood needs lived on in Ben as an adult.

Donna realized that she had developed a stalling strategy during childhood to resist a mother who was angry and constantly nagged her about time and hurrying. Knowing that Ben would judge or nag her if she was late, she unconsciously used her childhood resistance strategy to rebel and stall on her way home—to punish Ben for his anger.

When Ben and Donna became aware that their choices and reactions were being orchestrated by inner five-year-olds still stuck in the past, they learned to take over as adults and make conscious agreements that served them both.

The most important change was a tender respect between them for their mutual wounding and childhood strategies—and a willingness to honor those wounds while staying clear about who was in charge of their adult lives.

FROM CHEMISTRY TO REAL LOVE

We all talk about wanting to be intimate with each other, but until we're taking these disowned parts and bringing them into our awareness—knowing they're all perfect—we're not being intimate with *ourselves*. We're not intimate with our own feelings. And then we say, "Why do I keep choosing people who aren't capable of intimacy?"

When we claim intimacy with ourselves, we have no concern whatsoever about being intimate with someone else—and that's when we find people who are capable of intimacy.

I once had a client who was a matchmaker. She gave people exhaustive questionnaires. She interviewed them at length to find out all their interests. She knew everything about what people *said* they liked and wanted. Then she matched those profiles and sent them out with each other.

Invariably, they came back and said, "Well… it was nice. We had a nice dinner, but there was just no chemistry. No spark. No juice. They're a nice person, but I'm looking for the juice. I'll know when I find that juice."

What they were actually looking for was mutually compatible pathology juice.

Mutually compatible pathology juice comes with this mindset: *I'll do anything for this person. I'll do anything to hold on to this relationship. I'll lie, I'll manipulate my reality,*

I'll jump through any hoops they need me to. I've got to hold onto it because if it's taken away from me, it'll rip my soul apart. Without them I'm empty and alone. I'm incomplete.

The kind of chemistry we're used to thinking of as love is not love at all. It's fear. Fear that we're not going to be able to hold on to the commodity of love. Fear that we're not whole and we need someone else to complete us.

If we could learn to turn to each other and say, "I fear you so much," that would be a lot more true than "I love you so much."

In the old dream, "I love you so much" really means: "Please don't leave me. Please accept me. Please don't take away the commodity of love and attention I've been receiving from you. What do I need to do? What's the bargain?"

It's not love until we are loving ourselves, intimate with ourselves, and embracing ourselves in our totality. From that love, we can go out and meet *in love* with someone else—not falling in love through mutually compatible wounds, but as two whole people entering the state of love together. Not *with* each other as a source, but *in love together* as a shared experience.

That is love. That is divinity expressing itself through us. And that brings us back to Agreement Number Three: **I am whole and complete within myself, and I don't need anybody or anything to complete me.**

When we make that agreement with ourselves, we start rescuing, reuniting, and loving the parts of ourselves that were forced to split off when we were little. We actually do the work to become what we're agreeing that we are—whole and complete within ourselves.

From that place of acceptance and respect, we can make clear agreements about what we want, what we need, and how to make our relationships work.

Your Challenge:

1. **Make a list of any habits or characteristics of others that irritate you or that you judge.** Can you accept those habits or characteristics as reflections of your own disowned parts—and begin to accept them in yourself?
2. **Explore how childhood agreements, experiences, or survival strategies might be operating in your current relationships.** If they are, are you willing to make new agreements that support your adult love relationship? Write down those new agreements and practice living them until they become real for you.

Chapter 8
Agreement #4: The Truth Is More Important Than the Outcome of the Relationship

"Emotions are not a problem to be solved. They are a gift."

— *Allan*

THIS AGREEMENT IS ONE OF THE MOST RADICAL, BECAUSE for most of us, **truth was never safe**. Growing up, we learned that speaking our truth—especially when it was uncomfortable, emotional, or contradictory—could lead to rejection, punishment, silence, abandonment, or shaming.

So we adapted. We learned to tell people what they wanted to hear and edited ourselves to preserve the connection. We swallowed our truth in the name of peace, performance, or survival. And what happens when you do that for long enough? You forget how to be honest, even with yourself.

THE TRUTH BENEATH THE STORY

When I talk to people about "the truth," I often discover that they don't actually know what their truth is. The truth I'm talking about is emotional truth. The felt truth. The truth that lives in the body, not in the story.

Why is it so crucial to express your "feeling truth" in a relationship? The short answer is because expressing this kind of truth is one of the most intimate things you can do. It can be even more intimate than sex. This kind of truth-telling is what Jesus said "sets you free." The emotional truth has the power to create deep understanding, empathy, and an opportunity to fall even deeper into Love together.

WHAT INTIMACY REALLY IS (AND WHY WE'RE SO AFRAID OF IT)

Relationships suffer because of fear of intimacy.

You might be thinking, "No, that's not true! I'm not afraid of intimacy, I *want* intimacy!" Perhaps it will help if I define what intimacy means in the context of our sharing here.

When my dictionary defines intimacy, it begins with "a close personal relationship," and after a few less interesting ideas, ends with "sexual intercourse (used euphemistically)." Unfortunately, the same dictionary does not define "euphemistically," but basically it means using mild language to tone down something harsh or offensive. So, we use the word "intimate" as a way of obliquely referring to sex, or a close personal relationship.

My definition of intimacy is a little different.

I would like to redefine intimacy as "a willingness to be open and present and share ourselves with others." When two people can share this openness and presence, they can be said to have "an intimate relationship."

It is an unfortunate result of our childhood domestication that most of us are afraid of being seen. Our parents saw us, in our first close personal relationships, and rejected us as not good enough, not smart enough, too smart for our britches, not quiet enough, too loud, bad singers, or whatever particular set of standards of Good and Bad they were dreaming. Our worst offenses were usually related to free expressions of our emotions. We cried, laughed, sang out, jumped on things and ran in joy, pouted, and yelled in anger.

When we learned those emotional expressions were not acceptable ("Go to your room until you stop that crying!"), we knew we had to deny them in order to survive as part of our families. In place of our denied truth, we mocked up the appropriate behaviors that would assure our acceptance. We learned to wear masks to please our caregivers so they would take care of us.

Now, as adults, we expect ourselves and our partners to be intimate, to reveal and share the truth as it arises in our feelings and emotions. Fat chance! Been there, done that!

Intimacy has become the most desired *and* dreaded part of human relationship. We want to be seen, known, appreciated, loved, and accepted—and yet the old fear of being judged and rejected is very strong, and most of us rely on our masks to substitute for real connection.

Is this making sense? Do you recognize it?

Very often at personal growth workshops, I create experiences where people look into each other's eyes. For many, it is a very uncomfortable exercise. If you are uncomfortable when someone gazes too long into your eyes, is it because you are afraid of what they might see or find out? Will they find out all the bad and undesirable feelings and behaviors that your Inner Judge criticizes you for—and then reject you? None of this is good or bad, right or wrong, or a spiritual success or failure—it's simply the truth of how each of us manages our levels of intimacy to stay comfortable.

When we are not afraid of intimacy, we are able to share the very feelings and emotions that we have repressed and denied for so long. We open ourselves to be seen without fear of being judged or rejected. We stay present in our experience of other people and their experience of us.

You may be asking, "But why would I want to share my feelings and emotions? Who cares?" Feelings are so powerful, and so valuable! Acknowledging our feelings leads to healing and unification in our humanness.

Feelings are also a built-in, God-given system for taking us to the right relationship, career, and life purpose. Feelings inform you and tell you about yourself—what you like and what you dislike—and ultimately guide you to the life you're meant to live.

This level of openness requires an intimacy with your *own* emotional truth, your willingness to accept it as it is, and the courage to share it with others.

EMOTIONAL INTIMACY WITH OURSELVES

My client Jennifer called me, upset because there were no "emotionally available men" out there. She had been in *so* many relationships, she said, waiting for a man who would be present and show his feelings. She told me that she was often fooled, thinking a particular man wanted to share with her in a deeper way, but soon realized he did not. "Is it true," she asked, "that all men are emotionally unavailable?"

I asked her, "What do you do when you realize your man is not available to you emotionally?"

"Well, I usually try to figure out what's wrong and how I can encourage him to tell me what's going on with him. But he just doesn't want to answer me," she said, followed by a sigh of resignation.

I understood her pain, because I have heard this story from many people, both men and women. They want someone to be open, to share feelings with them, and to be emotionally available. After many years of research, I have finally discovered the reason that so many people find themselves in relationships with an emotionally unavailable partner.

It is because they are emotionally unavailable themselves!

It seems obvious when I say it, perhaps, but many people do not want to acknowledge their own difficulty with emotional intimacy, but instead blame their partner (or lack of partner) for the problem.

When we find "love" in our adult lives, it triggers the fears and strategies we learned in childhood. If our early experiences taught us to be afraid of expressing our emotional reality, we will not feel comfortable—or even willing—to express ourselves freely in our adult relationships. We must relearn how to be emotionally present.

Since we have lost the connection between our emotions and our awareness (through rigorous self-training), the first step is to become aware that we have lost that connection. The next important step is to realize that without full awareness and expression of our feeling truth, we are not fully alive. We are using the strategies we learned in childhood to manipulate our reality to please other people, and we are not being ourselves.

Once you understand that you have lost that connection, and you are passionately willing to risk anything to restore it, you are on your way to emotional freedom. From there, you will attract the guidance and healing you need to tune into your body, open the connection to your awareness, develop a language for the emotional energy you experience, and share that truth with the ones you love. You may find old emotional baggage from the past mixing with your present reality, and that's okay. It is all you, and all true.

When you learn to discharge and clear the old angers, hurts, fears, and shames of childhood, you open more space for presence in the subtle feelings of each moment. They may arise simply as, "I like this, I don't like this. I want this, I don't want this."

The most important victory in this process *is developing emotional intimacy with yourself*—bringing that same willingness to be open and present to your own feeling truth in each moment. Whether we are men or women, unless we are present with ourselves in this way, we cannot expect to be attractive or attracted to people who are emotionally present with themselves.

Here's what I mean when I talk about "emotional intimacy with ourselves." What happened when you were around four or five years old, and you cried? According to my client, Dan, his father would say, "There's nothing to cry about." Or, "Nobody wants to hear you cry."

Over the years, Dan learned to keep quiet and not cry. If his girlfriend cried, he had no idea how to comfort her.

And on the rare occasions when he felt like crying, he was horrified and choked it down at the throat.

Emotional intimacy with ourselves means being willing to allow ourselves to feel and witness our emotions with compassion. It means we encourage ourselves to have the emotions so that we can fully heal.

In the animal world, when an antelope is singled out by a lion and chased within an inch of its life but escapes back to its herd, it trembles and shakes with fear for a few moments, and then goes back to grazing with the rest of its family. What is the shaking about? That is the antelope's body's way of discharging the emotional energy so that it can return to normal.

Many of my clients have said, "I'm afraid to let my sadness and grief out. It's been suppressed for so long, and it feels so big, that if I open the gates I'll start crying and never, ever stop." This is never true! Once you open the doors to allow yourself to feel your feelings, they wash over you and heal the trauma so you don't have to carry it anymore.

Being emotionally present with ourselves means we have to get comfortable riding on a small boat in the ocean of feelings within us. Once you can get comfortable with your own feelings of anger, fear, and sadness, you'll be able to communicate those feelings to your partner without denying them or feeling ashamed. You'll also be able to be 100% emotionally available to witness and accept your partner's feelings.

My client Jennifer came to learn that her issue was not with the men in her life, but with her own fear of emotional intimacy with herself. She has now learned to open with love to the Divine perfection of everything she feels, thinks, wants, needs, loves, desires, and fears. All of her relationships now reflect the emotional intimacy that she thought was missing in the world for so long. And she is in love with life.

This agreement that "the truth is more important than the outcome of the relationship" comes *after* "you are not responsible for other people's emotional reaction to your reality," because if you still believe you must manage how others feel, you will never tell this kind of truth. Without that freedom, you'll always twist your truth to protect the relationship instead of letting the relationship be shaped by your truth.

HOW WE LEARNED TO CUT OURSELVES OFF FROM OUR FEELINGS

When we were little, we were wide open. Alive. Electrical. Our bodies were moving, cooking, buzzing with sensation. We didn't know the difference between thinking and feeling because we weren't thinking. We were feeling. That's what little kids do.

And then the messages started coming in:

"If you don't stop crying, I'll give you something to cry about."

"Go in the other room with that pouting face—I don't want to see it."

"Quit running around being so damn happy. You're giving me a headache."

"No wonder I drink."

Every message was the same: Your feelings are not okay.

Slow down. Sit still. Be quiet. Don't interrupt the adults. Be seen and not heard.

We were innocent actors in life—knocking over a glass, hitting a baseball through a window, spilling something —and the reaction we got wasn't about what happened. It was about our emotional response to it.

If we were hurt or sad or angry or even too happy, someone told us it was wrong. Or they didn't have to tell us—we just *knew* it wasn't welcome.

Maybe one tiny sliver of an emotion was acceptable, and everything else had to be shut down. So we learned to become that one acceptable sliver. We learned to bargain for approval and love by shaping ourselves to fit what kept us safest.

And how did we do that? We cut ourselves off at the neck.

There was no way to stop the natural emotional energy rising in our bodies because it's simply the nature of being alive—so we jammed a block between our heads and our hearts. We learned to override the body so we could think, because thinking got us in less trouble. Thinking allowed us to figure out what they wanted from us.

Running to Mom crying because our brother hit us? Nope. That got us scolded. So the next time we got hurt, we stuffed it. We learned that the feeling itself—not what happened, but the *feeling*—was the problem.

Once we pushed those feelings down long enough, we lost access to them completely. So when someone asked, "How are you?" or "What's going on with you?" the real information wasn't available anymore. The channel was cut. We had to go up into the mind and mock up an emotional reality that would satisfy the moment. Our minds started creating stories and approximations to replace the truth our bodies once knew.

This is how the split began between the head and the body, between thinking and feeling. Nobody warned us that this was happening. Nobody said, "You're losing access to your emotional truth; let me help you reconnect."

Every strategy we built to survive childhood, every pattern of shutting down, avoiding rejection, staying safe, staying small, we carried straight into our adult relationships.

And then one day we "fell in love," quotes very much intended. The old bargaining began again, only this time with higher stakes.

She asks him, "Do you love me?" He says, "Oh yeah, sure, I *think* I love you. I mean… I hang out with you all the time, don't I? Maybe we should get married. Not right away, but someday…"

And she thinks, *Well… it's not exactly what I wanted. But it's something. It's the best thing I've got going. If I stick around, maybe he'll learn to love me the way I need.*

Does this sound familiar?

And then—ten minutes later, ten years later, or fifty years later—we wake up and ask ourselves:

What happened to me?

Where did I go?

When did I lose track of my truth?

We don't know what we want because the place where that information lives is inaccessible.

I was talking to a man recently who told me he wasn't sure about his relationship. He said, "We get along well. She's wonderful. But in my head, I'm making lists of pros and cons. I keep waiting for one of these lists to get longer than the other, so I'll finally know what to do." But the lists kept seesawing back and forth, and he could never get one far enough ahead to feel certain.

He was trying to decide *with his mind* if he was in love.

So I asked him, "Do you want her?"

And then... silence. A long silence. The answer wasn't in his mind. It was in his body—his heart and belly—and he'd been trained not to go there. He knew plenty of facts about her, plenty of qualities he liked and didn't like, but he didn't know the truth at the core: Do I want her?

Even more tragically, he didn't know *how* to know.

The channel to his emotional truth had been closed for years.

WHAT THE BODY HOLDS TOO LONG, IT TURNS INTO ILLNESS

Isn't it interesting that most chronic diseases people suffer from today aren't things we catch from each other? They arise in the body itself. Our own hearts attack us.

When you push emotional energy down into the body and hold it there against its will, it has to do something with that pressure. The body is alive. Feeling is energy. It wants to move. It wants to discharge itself.

Watch a little child who gets hurt and runs to their mother, sobbing. If the mother holds the child and creates a safe space, what happens? The child cries and cries until the feeling has moved completely through them. And when the process is finished, they hop down and—just like that—they're happy again.

Because our nature is happy.

The emotional wave rises, moves through, expresses itself, and is gone. That's healing. That's completion.

Now imagine a little boy who gets angry. "Mommy, I hate you!" he shouts, swinging his arms. If she knows what she's doing—if she doesn't take it personally and doesn't believe she caused his emotional reaction—she can say, "Wow, you're really angry at me. You have every right to feel that. Let's find a way for you to express it safely, because I'm not going to let you hit me."

So she hands him a plastic bat. He pounds on a pillow, yells, and moves the rage out of his body. Then he looks at his mother, present, connected, and says, "This is what I'm angry about." And now they can work with the truth.

But most parents don't do this because they think they're responsible for their child's emotions. They believe that if the child is angry, they must have failed. So they take the anger personally and shut it down, desperate to restore their image as a "good parent."

If you are a parent, please don't use any of this against yourself. We are all doing the best we can with the tools we have, the wounds we carry, and the beliefs we were given. None of this is material to judge ourselves with. This is material to **free** ourselves with.

RECLAIMING THE TRUTH WE LEARNED TO HIDE

Most of us, to some degree, block the natural expression of our emotions simply because we never had a container—a safe lap, a steady presence—where someone said, "Let it all out. I'm right here until you're done. And then we can talk."

In adulthood, that kind of container is almost nonexistent. We parent our own emotions the same way they were parented when we were little. We unconsciously collude with each other to keep doing it—damping down feelings, smoothing over discomfort, doing whatever we need to do so no one rocks the boat.

If our own tears are backed up inside us, someone else's tears threaten to open the floodgates. So we stop them quickly. We hand them a tissue, pat their back, say, "It's okay, it's okay," not to comfort them but to silence the stirring in ourselves.

Therapists do this too. I've busted many of them. Professionals who are uncomfortable with raw emotion interrupt it, analyze it, and talk people out of it—anything to avoid going there themselves.

Even in the world of healing, there are very few real containers—places where the body is allowed to release the energy it has held for decades.

Romantic relationships are no different.

BECOMING THE STUDENT OF FEELINGS

To share the truth of how we feel, without attachment to the outcome of a relationship, is one of my definitions of conscious relationship—but before we can do that, we have to know what we feel in the first place.

You feel emotions in your body. They rise up in your guts and your heart, and reveal themselves as tears, yelling, laughter, and many other physical expressions. Your opportunity is to recognize them as a gateway for entering an exploration of the stories you tell yourself. Love your emotions, no matter what they are.

If you are in a heated or hurtful exchange, you may need to simply excuse yourself to go within. This is your work. What are you feeling? Anger? Sadness? Hurt? Drill down, and see what feeling is underneath it. If you are angry, ask yourself what is beneath the anger. Drill down. Listen quietly within.

You may hear "hurt" is beneath the anger. Drill down again. What is under the hurt, giving rise to the hurt? Most people find that at the base of all their emotional reactions is fear.

There can be a different story at each level as you go deeper. You are angry because your friend didn't pay you back the money they borrowed from you. Story: "People should keep their word." You feel hurt. Story: "They don't think I am worth respecting enough to keep their promises." You find fear: "I am afraid it is true; I am not worth their (or anyone's) respect."

At every level, you can ask, "Is it true?" Is it true that people should keep their word? Do you? Is it true that they are not paying you because they don't think you are worthy of respect? Once you find the fear story, the question to ask yourself is, "Is it true I am not worthy of anyone's respect?" The ultimate fear story for most humans in our culture is our fear that we are not worthy of the love, respect, care, or approval that we try so hard to earn. It is a lie!!!

The New Story: It is a lie that we are not worthy of love. We are beautiful gifts from the Divine to creation. We *are* the very love that created us. We don't have to be *worthy* of love; it is our nature, our being, and our reason for Life.

LEARNING A NEW FEELING LANGUAGE

"I feel like..." is not a feeling. It is a judgment. If you want to get close to the truth, use this form: I feel. One word. Period.

"I feel sad."

"I feel angry."

"I feel scared."

"I feel grateful."

Anything more than one word usually means you've left your body and climbed back into your mind where the old stories and judgments live. Those stories create emotions, yes, but the story is not the feeling. When the story takes over, the truth gets buried under analysis, blame, and expectations.

A new client called to tell me that she and her new husband had a big fight because he wouldn't listen to her share her feelings. He said he was tired of being made wrong, and all she wanted to do was tell him how she felt. She asked me, in a very discouraged tone, "How can I get him to just listen when I try to tell him how he is making me feel, instead of arguing with me?"

I asked her to tell me about the conversation and what had happened. She said they were talking about some money issues they were having, and she said, "I feel like you are careless with our money and should talk to me about it more." He protested that he was not careless and told her, "I feel like you are always making me wrong," which of course she denied: "I am only expressing my feelings."

Through reading books, our therapy experiences, and even magazine articles, many of us were taught to speak "I" language and "feeling" language. The point of this language was to keep discussions and arguments on our side of the fence and be responsible for our part. It was a good idea, and is still an important skill in intimate relationships.

Unfortunately, many people missed the subtleties of "I feel" and continue to use the language of judgment and blame. These statements do not share feelings:

- "I feel like you are insensitive when you talk like that."
- "I feel like I don't matter to you when you don't pay attention to me."
- I feel like you're a jerk the way you talked to that waiter."
- I feel like I shouldn't be so angry."

Very few of us learned to speak clearly about our emotions and feelings. The statements in the above illustrations are actually descriptions of "thinking," not feeling.

So how can we learn to speak an emotional language again?

Learning to use the words in a more precise way is a good start. Only use "I feel" when you want to describe an emotional experience occurring *in your body*.

I asked my client what she was *feeling* when she was *thinking* her husband was careless with their money.

It took a bit of coaching to move her from her mind's thinking to her body's feeling, but in time she realized she felt *angry*! Now *that* is an emotional experience. "I feel angry!" describes the sensations in her body in that moment.

As she started appreciating the possibilities, she blurted out: "I get it! I could have said to him, 'I *feel* afraid when I *think* you are careless with our money!' Then maybe he wouldn't have felt I was making him wrong! Oh, wait, he didn't *feel* wrong, he... thought... no, he felt afraid... afraid I didn't love him, I bet. Oh, we were both afraid and didn't know it, and so we fought."

And new possibilities of feeling, sharing, and loving opened in their relationship.

You might *think* your partner is insensitive, and *feel* angry when that thought arises. You might *think (judge)* your partner is a jerk—but how does it make you *feel*? Becoming aware of this difference between thinking and feeling offers you both the opportunity to express a new kind of truth in your relationships.

THE LIE THAT BECAME AN ENGAGEMENT

Let me tell you a story from long ago that illustrates what happens when we don't have the inner permission to express our emotional truth in a relationship.

I was in college, following the script that had been programmed into me:

Go to junior college.

Transfer to a four-year school.

Pick a profession.

Become it.

Meet someone.

Get married.

Have kids.

Get a good civil-service job with benefits so you can be home, stable, and safe.

Somewhere along the way, I got engaged. I say "got engaged" because I sort of tricked myself into it. I didn't mean to, but it was the best deal I could come up with at the time.

I was living with my girlfriend, and in those days, it was pretty wild to live together without being married, so we had to keep it completely secret. The Vietnam draft was active. I wanted to stay in school, so I was trying my best to drag out my college years. I found out that if I took on a special project, I could delay graduating by a year. And since staying in school meant I didn't have to deal with the draft yet, that sounded like a great idea. So I took a semester off and did this project.

I was studying park management back then, and the project involved driving around the whole country visiting national parks and forests. Before that, I'd been fighting forest fires in the mountains with a buddy of mine, and the two of us had been talking about doing this school project together. So I told the woman I was living with that I was going on this road trip with my friend.

She got really scared. She said, "If you go, I want to go with you. And if you don't take me, I won't be here when you get back."

We were bargaining. I didn't know what to do. I had no skills for truth-telling back then. I didn't want her to come with me, but I also didn't want to lose her. I remember thinking, *What am I going to do?*

So I asked her to marry me. That made her happy, and then I went on the trip with my buddy. That's how I started digging the hole deeper and deeper, because none of it was the truth yet.

When I got back, I knew I didn't want to get married. But instead of saying that, we kept setting dates. We were still in college, so we said, "We'll get married at Easter." Then Easter would get close, and I would push it off until Christmas. And then Christmas would get close, and I'd push it off again. I just kept doing that.

Finally she said, "If you don't keep this date, then it's off."

So there it was—my out. But I still couldn't take it. I couldn't tell the truth. I had no permission inside myself to say, "You know, I really don't want to do this."

Nobody had ever told me that was allowed. Nobody had ever told me that was an option in life. So instead of telling the truth, I tried something else. I wanted *her* to break up with *me*. So I quit my job. She was working a few hours after school in a daycare, making a few dollars, and I started taking money out of her purse.

(I'm embarrassed to admit this even now.) I'd buy beer with it, and I wasn't even that fond of beer.

I'd buy a six-pack, pour most of it down the sink, and toss the empty cans on the floor. We had this big recliner, and I'd pour a little beer on myself for effect, drink maybe half a can, and then flop back in the recliner in the dark.

She'd come home and I'd mumble, "Hey, baby," like something out of a scene in a bad movie.

But she was very forgiving. She forgave everything. So I kept escalating it. It was the only idea I had. And she just kept forgiving me. She'd say, "You know, the wedding is in a few weeks. The presents are starting to arrive in the mail." And I was getting more and more scared.

Then one day she brought my suit out of the closet and said, "If you don't take this in and get it altered, you're not going to be able to get married in it."

And right then, I knew I had come to a line I couldn't go past. I just blurted out, "I can't do this!"

Of course it was horrible. It was painful. It was abrupt. I'd been going along and going along, still secretly hoping she'd reject me and break up with me and hate me, and then somehow I'd be okay.

Well, she did break up with me, and she did hate me. She moved out the next day, and I never saw her again. She told me she was going to move to Boston, which she said was the farthest she could get from me and still speak English.

That whole situation was an extreme example of how afraid I was to simply tell the truth about what was happening inside me. Everybody else's expectations were going one way, mine were going another, and I couldn't imagine going against the tide of their expectations.

FINDING THE REAL FEELING

Let me ask you something. In that whole story I just told —if you were me, and you were going to say, "I feel _____. Period." What would you put in that blank?

Imagine yourself in my place. Imagine your body. Imagine what I was going through. What is the honest feeling I could have spoken?

Most people say *scared* or *terrified*. "I feel afraid." That's the truth. Guilt comes up, too.

Guilt *sounds* like a feeling, but guilt is something we think about ourselves. It's a judgment. It's a story. That story can create a sensation in the body, but guilt itself isn't the primary feeling.

The same goes for shame. What people call *shame* is actually something else underneath. Shame itself is more of an idea. It's an evaluation. It's judging ourselves, which creates a feeling in the body.

If you go underneath shame, you'll usually find something more basic—anger, fear, or some combination of
them. If you look for what's underneath anger and
sadness, you come to fear. No matter what it is, underneath you'll find fear. If you inquire, "What's under this
anger?" The answer is almost always, "I'm afraid of
something."

So guilt and shame are real experiences. But what I'm
talking about is identifying the feeling that lives underneath them, which is what your body is doing. If I sit
down and say, "I'm so ashamed," that's me judging
myself. And the other person's job, then, is to say, "Oh
no, you're okay, don't feel that way." I've just turned
myself into the victim and invited them to take care of
my victim. That's different from saying, "I'm feeling
afraid."

I'm using very strict language here for a very good
reason—to separate feeling from thinking, and from
evaluating, judging, and blaming. It's tricky.

If I had sat down with my girlfriend and said, "I'm
afraid." Just that—one word, period—would have
opened a very different conversation. A *beautiful* conversation. Because that was the truth.

But if I had said, "I feel like you're railroading me into
getting married," then I would have been judging her.
Blaming her. And she would have had to defend herself:
"No, I'm not. You wanted this. You said you wanted to
get married."

Can you feel the difference? "I'm afraid" opens a door. "I feel like you're railroading me," slams one shut.

I wasn't just afraid; I was *terrified*. I was terrified I was about to be swept into something I knew wasn't right for me.

Years later, I talked to my mother about it. She said, "You know, you wrote letters home during that time saying you thought she was kind of forcing you into it, and you didn't really want to do it. But you kept inviting us, so we were going to come." I had two totally different realities going on. On one hand, I was writing to my parents saying, "This doesn't seem right." And on the other hand, I was saying, "Okay, I'll do it." I was completely split, without any understanding of what was happening inside me.

AN EXAMPLE OF A CONVERSATION THAT SHARES FEELINGS AND BRINGS PARTNERS CLOSER

This is pretty sophisticated and will take practice. Both people in this conversation are drilling down through their emotions, finding the stories that live underneath the feelings and revealing them to each other.

"I feel afraid."

"Why?"

"When you told me earlier how you spent our money, I got scared because I thought it meant you didn't care about planning for our future or retirement. I was telling myself a story that it meant we would never have enough, that we would struggle like I watched my parents struggle with money. I got scared that it meant you weren't taking me or our children into consideration."

"That's not true at all. I do care. I feel angry that you think I wouldn't take care of our family."

"Now I feel even more afraid, because you're angry. I didn't mean for you to get angry."

"I know. The anger just rose up. Underneath my anger is the fear that I'm failing to take care of you. When you're afraid, I feel afraid that I'm not doing my job as a man to protect you. I worry that you're right about me, that I'm not a responsible man or father. And if that's true, then I tell myself it means I'm not worthy of your love. And if I'm not worthy of your love, I'm afraid that you'll leave me someday... and no one will love me. And I'll be alone, and die."

"Oh, that's not true! I do love you! I love you so much. I just want us to be on the same page with our finances."

"I want that too. What agreement can we make about money that will make us both feel comfortable?"

Do these types of conversations actually take place between people? YES! I have witnessed them hundreds of times in my work with couples. This is the kind of inner inquiry that's allowed to happen when people are comfortable with their feelings as they arise in their bodies.

If you think the husband's fear of dying was a bit far-fetched, it's not. I can tell you that every fear you have, if you drill down deep enough, leads to death. Try it. What are you afraid of right now in your life? Are you nervous about your finances? Are you afraid your partner might leave you? Ask yourself what you are afraid of if your fear comes true.

ALL FEARS LEAD TO A FEAR OF DEATH

Here's an example from one of my workshops. I was looking into the eyes of one of the participants, and she looked away and said, "For some reason, it makes me nervous when you look into my eyes like that."

"Why?"

"I don't know… I'm afraid you're going to see something stupid or bad about me."

"What are you afraid will happen if I see something 'stupid or bad'?"

"It will mean that it's true. There's something wrong with me."

"Okay, so what are you afraid of if there's something wrong with you?"

"That everyone will see it."

"What are you afraid of if everyone sees there is something wrong with you?"

"It will mean I'm not a good person and I'm not worthy of love."

"What are you afraid of if you're not a good person and not worthy of love?"

"I'll be rejected and alone."

"What are you afraid of if everyone rejects you and you're alone?"

"I'll be cast out of society, I won't have what I need, and... I'll die!"

It always pops up sooner or later. So just know that when you are scared in your relationship, the fear belongs to your inner four-year-old, who knows that if she is rejected and cast out of the family, she will die.

Your fear of the relationship ending is really a fear of death. The adult part of you knows that you won't die, but the little child part within has no idea. It's up to you to reeducate the child part inside. Tell him that HE is the source of love in his life. Tell him the truth about love, that he is love itself!

Embrace those old, disowned parts of yourself that are in the shadow so you can love and accept your partner and all of her ways of being in the relationship that you used to judge.

Explore your feelings and learn to become comfortable with them as they arise in your body. This is intimacy with our own emotions. Then take that intimacy into your relationships and share yourself with your loved ones.

I have faith in you, as life, as love, as unconditional acceptance.

FIVE COMMON STRATEGIES TO AVOID INTIMACY

Now that you know what real intimacy is about and why we avoid it, I'm outlining the five most common strategies I've seen couples use to avoid intimacy with each other. See if you can recognize any strategies you or your partner may unconsciously be using to avoid being seen.

1. Stay very busy. Always make sure you don't have time to sit, be present, and share with your beloved. Projects are more important than people. Focus on getting a lot of things done and done well. If you can sacrifice yourself in the process, you can make the other person feel guilty for complaining about your lack of presence.

2. Judge the other person. Whether it is out loud or silently to yourself, make sure you find and illuminate their faults. This will justify your not wanting to be present with them. It also serves to validate your superiority. When you rise above them, you don't need to be intimate.

3. Be a caretaker of others. Caretake to hide. You really *want* to be intimate, but you are needed elsewhere. When the chores are done, the kids are in bed, all your needy friends have been heard and consoled, the old dog is spoon-fed, *and* the whales are saved, *then* you will have time to go for a walk, take a weekend off together, or sit and talk.

4. Make yourself less attractive to avoid intimacy. Many people unconsciously adopt habits that dull their vitality, neglect their appearance, or compromise their health as a way to create distance.

This is not about beauty standards or trying to be "acceptable." I am not suggesting that anyone needs to look a certain way to be lovable. What I am pointing to is a subtle avoidance strategy I've seen in both men and women. When intimacy feels threatening, the body sometimes participates in pushing the other person away.

This can show up as neglect, overindulgence, withdrawal from self-care, or habits that slowly dim aliveness.

5. Do whatever it takes to avoid being seen and known. Drink a bit too much wine at dinner and fall asleep on the couch. Work late. Make sure all conversations are intellectual, scientific, or political—not personal.

Remember, you need to call a friend, check your email, or finish your novel. Read to the kids and fall asleep on their bed. Be angry, depressed, or stay in La-La Land. Tell jokes, gossip, teach or preach—anything but be real.

If you recognize some of these strategies as belonging to you or your partner, fear not. It's all due to the fear of intimacy (which you now know is the fear of being seen and rejected). With this new knowledge, you can begin to heal the emotional trauma of rejection from childhood and explore being more open and present with your own emotions and with a partner, too.

In the next chapter, we'll explore what true happiness really is and how it grows in direct proportion to the love that you give.

Chapter 9

Agreement #5: The Amount of Joy in Your Life is Equal to the Amount That You Love

"The love flowing out of you as acceptance of what is connects you with Life as the Divine Source, filling your heart with a joy and abundant happiness that can never be taken from you."

— Allan

TRUE HAPPINESS COMES FROM LOVE COMING OUT OF YOU.

We probably have as many different definitions of happiness as we have people on Earth, so I'm going to give you mine so we're on the same page. When I talk about happiness, I'm talking about *not suffering*.

We have two possibilities: we can be happy, or we can suffer.

So let me define suffering. Suffering is the experience we have when we think of ourselves as a victim. When we perceive ourselves as being victimized, we're suffering. And when we're suffering, we're not happy.

When we're free from suffering—which means we're free from seeing ourselves as victims—we're happy.

THE DIFFERENCE BETWEEN PAIN AND SUFFERING

There is also a very important distinction between **pain** and **suffering**.

As human beings, we will experience pain—physical pain and emotional pain. There is no avoiding it. We will lose people we love. Our bodies will get hurt. Things will happen that are painful. That is part of being alive.

But pain is not the same as suffering.

Suffering is what happens when we *tell stories* about the pain. Suffering is what happens when we judge the experience, judge ourselves, or decide that what is happening should not be happening.

We can experience pain fully—deep physical pain, deep emotional pain—and still not suffer.

That doesn't mean we're "happy" in a superficial way. I'm not talking about pretending everything is fine. I'm talking about a deeper happiness—the kind that is free from suffering even while grief is present, even while pain is moving through the body.

For example, you stub your toe in the dark at night. You can say, *"I'm so clumsy! I'm so stupid! Why do I always do this?"* That's judgment. Now you're suffering.

Or you can stand there in the dark and say, *"Wow. **That is pain.**"* And just experience it.

The pain moves through you. Your awareness is aware of the pain. There is sensation, intensity, energy—but no story, no victim, and no judgment layered on top of it.

When we stop telling ourselves the story—*this shouldn't be happening, this is unfair, why me*—we stay in our true nature even in the presence of pain. Grief can move. Physical pain can move. And love can keep flowing out of us.

You can stay what I call *happy* because you are not suffering.

Let's imagine you're in a relationship, and you come home one day to a note on the kitchen table that says, "I'm out of here."

Of course there's going to be pain.

You might be angry. You might be raging. You might be terrified. You might collapse and cry. All of that can be present.

If you're not making yourself wrong for those feelings…

If you're not making the other person wrong…

If you're not telling yourself stories about what it means…

And instead you're simply saying, *"This is a perfect unfolding of the universe in this moment, and I am going to experience all of it, including these emotions..."*

Then you can have your pain **and** your happiness at the same time.

Not a denial of pain or a spiritual smile pasted over grief. But a full, present, alive, human experience where the pain moves through you, and suffering does not arise.

When you are not a victim of your story...

When you are not judging the experience...

When you allow what is...

Then your true nature is still there.

And your true nature is happy.

In the first agreement (You Are the Source of Love in Your Life), we saw that we came into this world not judging, not suffering, not blaming. We came into this world as happiness. When we were infants, we were not making others wrong. We were not saying, "This isn't fair. Why me? Poor me."

No six-month-old is lying in the crib thinking, *"Look at these people. This isn't fair. Why did I have to be born into this family?"* We do that when we're forty-five in therapy, but we don't do it when we're six months old.

We don't have any clue about suffering when we're little. We're not ashamed of our bodies. We're not ashamed of what we feel, what we think, what we want, what we're attracted to, or what we're repelled by. We're present in the moment. We're magic. The world is magic to us, and we're happy.

As our domestication begins, we're taught about judgment, and that's when the suffering begins. Whenever there's judgment, there's a victim. Whenever there's a victim, there's suffering.

Happiness is the absence of suffering. Happiness is our nature. We learned to suffer because we learned to be victims. We learned to judge, to be judged, and to be afraid of judgment.

So to be happy, all we have to do is quit seeing ourselves as a victim. To quit seeing ourselves as a victim, all we have to do is quit judging ourselves, quit believing other people's judgments of us, and quit judging others.

JUDGMENT CREATES VICTIMHOOD

If we're standing in line at the DMV, angry and judging the DMV, it's because we're perceiving ourselves as a victim of the DMV. Do you see how that works?

Any time we're judging something "out there"— another person, an event, a war, a president—anything at all, we're perceiving in some way that we're being victimized by it.

Sometimes it's easy to see. If it's a long line, that's pretty obvious. But if we're judging something a politician did, it might take a minute to ask, *How am I being victimized by that?*

What we usually discover is that we're afraid. And if we're afraid, we're a victim. Or we're projecting that we're going to be a victim because we're afraid of what the politician is doing.

So if we're judging *out there*, we're creating a victim *in here*. If we're judging ourselves, we're creating a victim within. And if we believe someone else's judgment of us, we're creating a victim within, too.

Even if we believe we are the perpetrator—if we think we've hurt someone else—we judge ourselves for being a perpetrator and end up victimizing ourselves.

Any time we're feeling victimized, we're not happy. We're suffering.

If we've learned to make the other agreements we've been talking about in this book, we have the power to end judging altogether.

We wouldn't be judging out there, because we would know that we are perfect the way we are—because we are love. We are the Divine expressing itself as this unique manifestation, once in the lifetime of the universe.

YOU ARE THE ONLY ONE LIKE YOU EVER MADE

This is the first *you* since people crawled out of the swamp and started walking around. The first one exactly like you ever made. And I'm pretty sure it's the last one. No matter how many humans are born in time, there's never going to be another one like this.

So what's there to judge? What's there to make wrong? If you're the only one like this that has ever existed, there's no criterion to judge you against. You're unique.

It's like snowflakes judging other snowflakes.

"Ew, I don't like this snowflake. It should be like that one."

"I wish all snowflakes were the same."

"Your snowflake is too small."

"I'm jealous because your snowflake is bigger than mine."

And by the way, we're here for about as long as a snowflake, too.

We are unique expressions of Divinity—this mysterious life force that springs into life through some unknowable conception process, and then somehow knows how to mature itself from a single cell through puberty all the way to who you are now, without you having any idea how to do that.

You didn't wake up one day and say, *"I'm fourteen. Time to start growing armpit hair."* Thank God we're not in charge of all that. We wouldn't have time to learn algebra.

We are unique expressions of the Divine, and there's nothing to judge about us.

There's no book. There's no God with a clipboard. There's no Santa Claus. There's no one making a list and checking it twice to see if you're naughty or nice— deciding whether you get a stocking full of gifts or a lump of coal. No heaven-and-hell reward system. No purgatory.

That's all made up. When we're little, eventually someone tells us there's no Santa Claus—or we figure it out ourselves, and they say, "Okay, but don't tell your little sister." But no one ever says, *"Psst... There's no God like that either. There's nobody watching you, waiting to punish you."*

Humans created God in their own image: judging, rejecting, approving, rewarding, punishing. This God is also loving and kind and omnipotent and loves all of his children... *if* they follow his rules.

And of course, every God has different rules. That's why we have wars.

So if you truly recognize that you are unique, divine, and perfect exactly the way you are, then your self-judgment ends. And I guarantee you this: when your self-judgment ends, your judging of the world ends too.

You can't totally accept yourself and still believe there's something wrong with anybody else. If you see that *you* are absolutely divine and perfect, you have to recognize that perfection in every other unique, beautiful expression of the Divine.

Every tree. Every president. Every accident. Everything in the universe.

Even if you turn on the radio and they say there's an asteroid coming that's going to annihilate the planet, you still have a choice. You can tell yourself a story about how perfect that is—and be annihilated in perfect, open love.

Or you can tell yourself some other story. Because that, too, would be perfect. Do you see?

So first, we bring awareness to this. Then we make the agreement. And then we do whatever it takes to prove it to ourselves. Most of us have spent many, many years proving the opposite.

We've been proving to ourselves that we're flawed, wrong, broken, or not enough.

Often, we think the judge inside is trying to help us. We think it's trying to make us happy by pointing out everything that's wrong with us—so we'll shape up, do what we're supposed to do, and *then* we can be happy.

It's never worked.

If you know that you are perfect exactly the way you are, and you stop judging, then you will never be victimized. And if you are never victimized, your true nature is free to express itself.

Your true nature is happiness. Joy. Delight. That is what you are.

Happiness is the natural expression of the Divine moving out of you—accepting everything exactly the way it is. If you walked out into the world accepting everything exactly as it is, I think you'd be pretty happy.

There would be nothing to disturb you. Nothing to throw you off. Nothing to trigger unwanted emotional reactions. Because everywhere you looked, you would see divine perfection unfolding. And since you would recognize the Divine *out there*, and know that you are the Divine *in here*, then every place you looked in creation would become a mirror, reflecting back to you the divine perfection that you are.

That's easy to do with a tree. A lot of us go to nature because it acts like a mirror, and we go, *Ahhh*. It's not judging me. There's a majesty there. A presence. An aliveness. And it's just there. It doesn't ask anything of us. We don't have to bargain for its attention. We don't think it's judging us.

We might still judge it, but it's easy to see the Divine in certain aspects of nature. It's harder to do with people.

I remember Ram Dass telling a story a long time ago about his altar. He had pictures of his gurus on it, and then he had a picture of Caspar Weinberger, former Secretary of Defense under President Ronald Reagan.

Someone asked him, "Why would you have *him* on your altar?"

And Ram Dass said, "Well… divinity. Divine master. Love you."

And he'd move along the altar, guru after guru, "Divinity… divinity… divine master… love you…" And then he'd get to Caspar Weinberger's picture, and he'd say, "Ah… divinity."

If I can learn to see the Divine there, then the Divine can be mirrored back to me as the Divine. But the minute I say *bad person*, the minute I judge, I'm back in victim mode, and I've lost my happiness.

You can watch this in real time. Pick up the newspaper. Turn on the news. Can you stay out of judgment? Out of fear? Out of rejection? Can you stay present with everything that's happening in the world and the universe?

Because if you can, it will make you happy all the time. Love will come pouring out of you as acceptance.

Remember what I said at the beginning: true love is acceptance.

We don't actually know whether the world will improve—but we do know that *our* world will improve. And that matters, because if we try to do this in order to fix the world, it means we're judging the world. And the moment we're judging the world, we're back in victim mode. We're acting out of fear instead of love.

CHOOSING ACTION WITHOUT ATTACHMENT

Take environmental activism as an example. Groups like Greenpeace do a lot of good. They bring awareness. They shine a light on important issues. And yet, much of that action is often fueled by judgment. *"This is wrong. This shouldn't be happening. We have to stop these bad people from doing this bad thing."* So even when the intention is good, the underlying energy can still be victimhood—fear, anger, and judgment rather than love.

So the real question becomes: **How do we stay passionate about the things we care about while acting from love and acceptance instead of fear?**

We assume that whales are meant to exist forever. We assume rainforests are supposed to last forever. We assume ice caps should always remain at the poles. And when something threatens those things, we decide it's bad.

But how do we know what the world is *supposed* to look like?

We want it to stay the same. Even if we never go to Bodega Bay to watch the whales, we like knowing we *could*. It feels right to us. But that doesn't necessarily mean that's where the larger unfolding of the universe is headed.

Dinosaurs came and went over millions of years. Now they're gone. Was that bad?

If Greenpeace had been around back then, they probably would have saved them—and then we'd have a serious problem because dinosaurs would be walking around crushing our cars. We'd have to wipe most of them out anyway and keep a few in zoos. So maybe it's a good thing the dinosaurs are gone. Now we have lizards and toads. Much more manageable.

The truth is, we don't really know what's right or wrong in the big picture. We're hurtling through space on a ball of molten rock, traveling at over 800 miles an hour around an exploding ball of gas that we affectionately call "the sun," and our hair doesn't even get messed up. We have no idea what's going on here. We take a tiny slice of the universe—a war, a species going extinct— and we say, *"This shouldn't be happening."*

I'm not saying we shouldn't care. I'm not saying we shouldn't be moved. Since we don't know how it's supposed to be, why not choose to come down on the side of saving the whales?

Choose your action. Be passionate about your action. But don't be attached to the outcome.

Act from love, not from judgment. From acceptance, not from fear. That's where true happiness stays intact. Then you can be in love, because you no longer need to make anyone wrong.

You could go to the people who are cutting down the rainforest and say, *"I love you. Let's talk about alternatives."* That isn't happening very much yet. Most environmental activism is still fueled by anger—*tree-huggers versus loggers*, us versus them.

Love doesn't require agreement, and it certainly doesn't require judgment. The moment we make someone wrong, we've lost our happiness. We've stepped back into victimhood.

True happiness is love coming out of you. The amount of joy in your life is equal to the amount that you love.

Chapter 10
Returning to the Dream of Heaven on Earth

"The purpose of our lives is to be happy."

— *Allan Hardman, quoted by the Dalai Lama*

As you've journeyed through these pages, you've begun to loosen the old agreements that shaped the dream of your life. You've seen the beliefs you inherited without your consent, the emotional patterns that you adopted, and the masks you learned to wear to feel safe. You've remembered truths that were always yours.

You came into this life as Love. You learned fear. And now you are remembering Love again. If you take nothing else from this book, let it be this:

You are the source of Love.

You are not responsible for the emotional reactions and dreams of others.

You are whole and complete within yourself.

You have permission to feel and speak the emotional truth moving through you.

The more love that flows out of you as acceptance, the happier you become.

These agreements are not rules. They are invitations back to yourself.

The New Relationship offers a strengthening of your awareness so that you can walk through this world with your heart open and your truth unhidden.

When you meet others from this place, you *recognize* each other—two whole beings choosing to walk side by side, without fear and without demands.

This is love without fear. This is freedom.

And because this freedom begins in you, it radiates into every relationship you have, including the most important relationship of all—the one you have with yourself.

I invite you to dream consciously.

Dream with the awareness that everyone you meet is doing their best inside their own dream.

Dream with compassion for the little child within you who only ever wanted to be loved.

Dream with joy, because joy is your natural state when you stop resisting life.

Dream with Love—because Love is what you are.

THE NEW RELATIONSHIP

Let this moment be your awakening.

Let this breath be your return to yourself.

Let this life be the Dream of Heaven on Earth.

Dream with me one more time.

Dream the dream where you are free.

A Final Blessing

Divine Presence, as we come together to
    deepen our awareness of Your presence in
    our lives—as Life, as Love, as Spirit, as
    God, by the many names we know You—
help us, Divine Presence, to know that You are
    who we are.
You are Us at the very core of our being.
As we call out to You and ask You to share
    Your love with us, to teach us how to love
    ourselves the way You love us—
Love without conditions,
Love without obligations,
Love without bargains—
We say: help us.
Show us how to love ourselves the way You
    love us.
Help us remember that the Love that You are is

*the Love that we are, and that there is no
separation.*

*Help us remember that the one thing that You
are is in and through every manifest part of
creation.*

There is only one of Them...

And we are That.

*Help us to know that truth, to stand in that
truth, to honor the truth that we are Love,
that we are Life.*

*And as You—as that Life and that Love—rise
in us, expressing Yourself as the unique
human each one of us is, help us to honor
that expression...*

*To clear the stories, to stop fighting the truth,
and to allow the truth that You are, that we
are, that I am, that It is...*

*To flow through us and out into the world, to
light the world with Your love.*

*As we go into our separate homes, to our part-
ners or alone—it does not matter, because
we know that we are that life force...*

And we are never alone.

*As we open to that truth, as we experience that
truth, we know that the abundance that
You are—as Divine Presence, as us—fills
our lives with everything we need effort-
lessly, because there is no separation.*

And we dream a dream of that Oneness.

*We dream a dream of loving ourselves as
perfect beings of Light, of Love, of Life.*

*We see the perfection, and we awaken in the
  morning carrying that dream into our
  lives, into our day, radiating that Divine
  Presence, knowing that It is expressing
  through each of us perfectly…*

*Seeing the unique expression in everyone else,
  and seeing that one truth of the Divine
  Presence in everyone else.*

*And as we go on with our lives, I name that
  this truth lives in each one of us.*

*I name it for myself, and I name it for everyone
  here.*

And it awakens into a new dream.

And so it is.

— Allan Hardman

Epilogue

ALLAN WANTED TO WRITE THIS BOOK FOR OVER TWENTY years. He was so creative, so brilliant, and so devoted to exploring and sharing ideas that he never quite got around to it. Fortunately, his teachings were preserved in the form of written articles and recorded classes on the subject, all of which made this book possible.

For years, Allan offered Thursday evening talks in Santa Rosa, California. I was his assistant then, and felt blessed to sit in the room and witness these teachings unfold. His words created real healing—not just for me, but for everyone who came to listen. By the time the evening ended, the energy in the room was always transformed.

Allan was a master of unconditional love. He never abandoned anyone. It didn't matter how difficult, wounded, or needy someone appeared. Many who came to him were so lost and hurt by their childhood experiences that their pain manifested in ways others didn't know how to handle.

Not Allan. He showered them with patience, presence, and belonging. Under his non-judgmental gaze, a person could begin loving and accepting themselves for the first time, having finally experienced what it felt like to be loved exactly as they were, with no expectation to heal or change.

The first time I saw Allan work, he held a grown man who sobbed in his arms. His love created a safe space for us to be vulnerable without shame. The parts of ourselves that we rejected, Allan accepted. That was his gift, and it's what made him such a remarkable guide.

It's also what made him a master of relationships. Allan did not disappear when love became difficult. He stayed present, honest, and available, loving without owner-ship and without using commitment as a substitute for truth. Instead, he lived the way he encouraged others to live: freely and passionately, without attachment to the outcome.

Allan was a teacher and guide, a healer and lover, a father figure, a brother, and a loyal friend. He was a Master of Love who made life on Earth feel gentler, kinder, and more bearable for hundreds of students and apprentices around the world.

To those of us who loved him, he was the love of our lives.

Jessica Varga McKay

About the Author

Allan Hardman (1942-2024) was an author, teacher, inspirational speaker, relationship coach, and Toltec Master who trained personally with don Miguel Ruiz, in the tradition of *The Four Agreements*. He was the author of *The Everything Toltec Wisdom Book* and co-author of *The Heart of Healing* and *Healing the Heart of the World*.

Allan taught in Sonoma County, CA, in the summer, and from his "House of the Eagles" in the beach village of Chacala, Nayarít, Mexico in the winter. He supported clients and apprentices all over the world through his Toltec Apprentice Community Online (TACO). He guided many spiritual journeys to the Toltec Pyramids at Teotihuacán, Mexico, and other sacred sites in Peru.

Allan's passions were conscious relationships and Toltec wisdom. His specialty was helping people identify and change the beliefs, agreements, and lies that limited their lives.

Learn more about Allan and his work at Joydancer.com.

About Spirit Wing Press

Spirit Wing Press is dedicated to publishing legacy books that heal, uplift, and change lives. It works with spiritual authors to bring their teachings into the world, honoring each voice with integrity, care, and respect. Each book is stewarded with a commitment to the lasting impact of the medicine it offers.

SpiritWingPress.com